"A must-have guide for any aspiring mobile food entrepreneur. From business planning and financing to licensing, this book covers it all!"

– Meghan Blake-Horst, Street Vending Coordinator, City of Madison, WI

"This book fits the needs of an aspiring food truck entrepreneur. It could be their bible, helping them to be profitable, have a more enjoyable life experience and saving them many mistakes and much grief. I love it that it doesn't sugar coat the risks or the amount of sweat and hard work it takes. It has academic rigor and contains practical down-to-earth advice."

— Kevin Appleton, Madison College Continuing Education Food & Beverage Program Director

FUELING A FOOD TRUCK

Kay-Tee Olds

ISBN (print): 978-0-578-51318-8
ISBN (ebook): 978-0-578-51319-5

Introduction

Everything that can go wrong will go wrong if given the chance, according to Murphy's Law. From having a food truck recovered from two feet of mud, up a hundred-yard hill after a three-day festival to watching a tent canopy fly past the state capitol building as a storm rolls through an event, the life of a food truck owner can be filled with moments of sun-up comedic relief and late-night hysteria. And yet the thrill of creating something new, often from scratch—that brings smiles to self-proclaimed food critics and provides jobs to families—can be the best ride at the carnival.

Food trucks and various forms of mobile food apparatuses are populating the street corners around the country, and as they multiply, new entrepreneurs join the race for mobile gold. While some well-meaning entrepreneurs have already counted their losses, others are continuing to grow their mobile food businesses with success. Understanding the food truck craze, evaluating if it is a good fit, and planning for a realistic operation can be the difference between tears and triumph. There are common misperceptions about what it takes to start, operate, and exit a food-truck business. Just because someone makes a tasty taco or award-winning chili does not mean their business will be sustainable. Yet, it is possible to create a profitable and sustainable mobile food business. Success starts with treating it like a business rather than a hobby. That requires creating a plan, consulting subject-matter experts, and properly funding the business.

This book contains academic rigor and applicable real-world scenarios to help readers who may want to start a mobile food-vending business decide whether to start up—and if they do choose to start up, this book aims to help prevent some of the most common mistakes. It examines the opportunities and threats of the food truck industry while helping readers to apply the material to their pragmatic planning process. As outlined in this book, each aspiring food truck owner may be entering the race for a different reason and with various motivations or limitations. Identifying personal values is as an important part of the business planning process when developing such a microbusiness. Some readers may be more comfortable with their abilities in one area of the business than another, so this book is broken into sub-sections, to allow the book to be frequently referenced throughout the startup process. If readers work through each section of this book, using it as a guide to produce a business plan, they will be able to objectively evaluate the viability of their business concept and use the plan to procure funding for their startup.

Some food truck owners aspire to fine-tune their skills as business owners and chefs, to later start brick-and-mortars. And some restaurants are growing new streams of revenue by taking their food to the customer which means that established restaurants are also starting food trucks. In comparison to its brick-and-mortar counterpart, a food truck is a low-risk entry for someone to start a retail food business. During numerous casual conversations with food truck owners, I found that most food trucks startups range between $15,000 and $200,000 and do not require long-term contracts. The U.S. Chamber of Commerce Foundation expressed an approximate startup cost of $90,300, with the $300 representing the costs of licenses and permits.[1] As an industry that started and continues to grow extremely organically, without much hierarchy or structure to follow for new entrants, the navigation of such a space can be overwhelming for some entrepreneurs. A limited number of books have been published about food trucks, an even smaller number of accredited training programs exist, and the rules of the game are continuously changing. Many food truck owners and other stakeholders within the mobile food ecosystem acknowledge the frustrations and confusion that surround the changing regulations—or the lack of clear language in them. Unlike traditional retail businesses that may operate out of storefronts, mobile food businesses require additional permits, licenses, inspections, and often subjective reviews. Asking specific questions—seemingly too often—can save a lot of headaches and money for a business that exists in this ever-changing space.

Before writing this book, I founded a food cart that traveled throughout the state of Wisconsin, serving up Southern-inspired street fare from a six-by-ten-foot cart

---

1 "Will Regulations Cool the Red-Hot Food Truck Industry?" U.S. Chamber of Commerce Foundation. March 23, 2017. Access April 12, 2019. https://www.uschamberfoundation.org/blog/post/will-regulations-cool-red-hot-food-truck-industry.

that was fabricated from a Homesteader Trailer. My mobile food cart later grew into a food-contract provider and then a full-service catering business. Sure, I had taken courses about business management and even small business startup during my various chapters of life as a student, which eventually resulted in earning a Master of Business Administration. But there was not a course I could find in the Midwest at that time—and there were few books out there—that taught someone how to start a food truck. I used to joke with a now-retired vending coordinator that this (starting a food truck) would be a whole lot easier if everything you needed were in one place! Since the industry grew so organically, many cart operators learned the trade through self-taught experiences coupled with some friendly advice or sharp warnings from veteran cart owners. Now, as the curriculum creator and instructor of a college-level food truck startup program, I help aspiring entrepreneurs enter the food truck space with realistic expectations, knowing what questions to ask. Interviews with subject-matter experts and other research methods were coupled with first-hand experience to create this material. As a serial entrepreneur who has started organizations in various sectors and vastly diverse industries, I can attest that navigating the ever-changing rules and playing within the boundaries of a food truck require a great thirst for finding solutions. This form of microbusiness requires constant evaluation and pivoting to experience the raw realities of success. Imagine creating a new sauce while each day and each person touched by the business adds another ingredient, wanted or not, and stirs the pot a little more until that sauce is perfected.

Understanding the nuances of food trucks and the environment surrounding them can help future owners to minimize their losses and capitalize on a rapidly growing opportunity. Market research can uncover the significant opportunities and threats while entrepreneurs can define their own strengths and weaknesses. Market research can also help remove or validate assumptions during the startup process. Entrepreneurs entering the food truck scene represent a more diverse and less experienced population of business owners as-a-whole[2]. There is still a sense of pioneering when entrepreneurs must navigate a space that is becoming more regulated while receiving criticism for lacking clear parameters in many markets.

Lack of access to funding and business-management experience can be the largest roadblock faced by many food truck startups. Creating a business plan with appropriate depth and creating a support system of subject-matter experts can combat those challenges. While many food trucks are started with insufficient funding or personal funding solutions, there are other routes to consider that can open doors to future funding in case it is needed as the business grows. As the business matures or faces financial challenges, it becomes even more important than it was during the planning process to prepare cash-flow proformas and other valuable financial documents that can help a business owner to analyze the health of the business.

Despite the disadvantages that some entrepreneurs face

---

2 "Will Regulations Cool the Red-Hot Food Truck Industry?" U.S. Chamber of Commerce Foundation. March 23, 2017. Access April 12, 2019. https://www.uschamberfoundation.org/blog/post/will-regulations-cool-red-hot-food-truck-industry.

when starting this type of business, there are food truck owners in small towns and large cities alike who are creating sustainable businesses that can support livelihoods and have a positive impact on their communities. Life as a food truck owner is not usually easy, and that may be why it is important for operators to find a way to enjoy working through the constant barrage of situations that command unique solutions. For those who plan the work and work the plan in a way that does not sacrifice their personal values, the journey can be one of awakening and discovery.

Contents

Chapter One

Understanding the Food Truck Craze

Social, local, mobile is all the buzz for diners, so food trucks are in position to continue growing in popularity. As customers seek convenient, affordable, seemingly foodie menu options, the story is being told through the Gram. Posting a picture to Instagram while stopping by a food truck or snapping a filtered photo while devouring that deliciously messy BBQ slider from a red-and-white-checkered paper boat, customers continue to pay tribute to their beloved food truck chefs. Each customer is the current food critic as food trucks vie for accolades and a loyal following of customers. All that local fame and joyous independence is coupled with a lower financial risk to start a food truck, compared to the cost of a brick-and-mortar restaurant. It is no wonder so many aspiring entrepreneurs are attracted to this popular business model that is on the rise and growing faster than its brick-and-mortar counterparts.

Food trucks generate a triple-win in many communities. Mobile food-service growth outpaced brick-and-mortar restaurants by 1.1 percent in 2017 as it became a $2.7 billion industry. The industry of mobile food service, driven by food trucks and food carts, grew 300 percent over the previous three years.[3] The industry now employs over fourteen thousand workers in the US.[4] Researchers predict continued growth in the number of food trucks throughout the country, especially in suburban markets. While many are found in coastal areas, they have also appeared in many small towns and various urban cities. The visual of food truck continues to depart from the 1970's chuck wagons as the space continues to meet current customer expectations.[5]

Photo Source: Kay-Tee Olds, Opry, Nashville, TN, March 2019.

3   Food Truck Nation." Food Truck Nation. Accessed March 21, 2019. https://www.foodtrucknation.us/.

4   Galatro, Tori. "What Data Can Tell Us About The State Of The Food Truck Industry." FoodTruckr. September 06, 2018. Accessed March 21, 2019. https://foodtruckr.com/2017/09/what-data-can-tell-us-about-the-state-of-the-food-truck-industry/.

5   "What Data Can Tell Us About The State Of The Food Truck Industry."

Restaurants may view food trucks as competition and rally together to restrict locations or density to protect their livelihood. However, it is becoming more common for current restauranteurs to expand their reach by going to their customers, with the addition of a food truck. Four thousand food trucks and counting share the ability to be mobile and go to the customer, but they differ greatly from each other, as independent customization is a key attraction to such a venture. One food truck may be equipped as a seemingly standard carnival truck that serves freshly squeezed lemonade wherever the large audiences convene for festivals. The next apparatus may appear to be hand-crafted with a DIY approach and found serving up a single dinner shift of from-scratch recipes at a local neighborhood corner. Since most food trucks entering the market are independently owned, they can vary in appearance, operation, and menu as much as each owner is unique from another.

Where and Why

Street locations and corners account for 55 percent of reported sales revenue while construction worksites and industrial sites account for 15 percent, shopping malls 12 percent, and other locations, venues, and event centers account for 18 percent.[6] According to the Bureau of Labor Statistics, growth of food trucks can be correlated to growth in restaurant and catering businesses since areas that experience spikes in trucks, also have growth in their counterparts. Seattle, is an example of the finding that

---

6 "How to Start a Food Truck Business with No Money." ProfitableVenture. Accessed April 15, 2019. http://www.profitableventure.com/.

food truck growth does not automatically mean decline in restaurants since King County has a booming food truck scene and also has 16 percent restaurant growth since 2010.[7] Food deserts, such as a row of wine shops, welcome food trucks so customers can stay and enjoy themselves in the area without leaving for food. Then again, Seattle is also experiencing a unique collision of economic factors, where living wage continues to rise but not keep up with the inflated prices of living. Many restaurants attempt to combat the raised wages and protect their margins by charging customers a service fee at each table. Food trucks are often operated solely or in part by the owner, so owners' draws are dependent on net profit rather than hours worked, which is different than how an hourly employee is compensated on their paycheck. Growth of food trucks is not only happening in markets where such unique economic environments are experienced as in Seattle. Travis County, Texas is home of Austin, TX which is no stranger to the food truck scene. Restaurants climbed 18% as food trucks grew 600% in Travis County, Texas.[8]

Shifts in economic environments and customer demographics have changed the way people consume food. Millennials now represent a significant group of consumers. Born between 1977 and 1992, they have surpassed the baby boomers to become the country's largest living generation. According to the latest US Census report,

---

7   "America's Food-truck Industry Is Growing Rapidly despite Roadblocks." The Economist. May 04, 2017. Accessed March 21, 2019. https:// www.economist.com/graphic-detail/2017/05/04/americas-food-truck-industry-is-growing-rapidly-despite-roadblocks.

8   "America's Food-truck Industry."

the millennial generation now totals 83.1 million, which is one quarter of the US population.[9] Collectively, they boast a $250 billion purchasing power, which, along with the segment's size and their nearly obsessive use of social media, makes them strong influencers in today's food-service industry.

Like the demographics that make up food truck entrepreneurs, millennials are a more ethnically diverse population than earlier generations that previously drove the consumer demand of a market. That identity aligns with eating habits that have become increasingly influenced by cultures from around the globe. This diversity enables them to be more experiential with their dining habits and food choices, but conversely those same habits and choices have been affected by the increased requests for accommodation of their special dietary needs. Their diversity also drives the trend of global food experiences and the infusion of different culinary traditions, which aligns with a broader trend for a blending of local and global influences.

Social trends continue to affect customer demand and therefore menu creation. Locally sourced, fresh product that is free of GMOs (genetically modified organisms) has a value today much greater than it did in previous decades. The masses are now looking for small batch or foods that do not seem like they were prepared for the masses. While it may not be reasonably possible for a food truck to

9 US Census Bureau. "Millennials Outnumber Baby Boomers and Are Far More Diverse." The United States Census Bureau. January 19, 2018. Accessed March 21, 2019. https://www.census.gov/newsroom/press-releases/2015/cb15-113.html.

source everything locally due to availability or cost, the key for most buyers of local products is to source locally when they can. The same economic factors that receive a boost when local purchasing happens are often closely tied to the food truck or its stakeholders. Some buyers are looking outside of traditional distribution channels to source their products. Local produce auctions, other small-batch producers, and local businesses willing to team up are a few of the solutions a food truck may consider when looking for products that were not mass-produced or distributed.

Scope

This book is designed not just to arm aspiring entrepreneurs of food trucks with enough information to be dangerous but mostly to inspire the right questions to be asked. It was written by a food truck owner, for a food truck owner. Starting a food truck can emulate the early stages of numerous small-business start-ups with characteristics that cross borders and industries. The importance of identifying the motivations and limitations of the founder is not unique to this type of business but equally as relevant as the tactical considerations of building out a food truck apparatus or designing a menu that stretches the margins between expenses and revenue. While this book does not expand much beyond the startup process, it challenges the reader to focus on building a strong foundation to the business that can sustain it through the inevitable pivotal moments that will later be encountered—while placing value on genuine leadership and leading toward the exit strategy.

Food truck, *food cart*, and *mobile food services* are used interchangeably throughout the book in reference to general mobile food services. However, the differences between the models should be considered before starting such a business, and the considerations for such a decision will be covered in Chapter Two. Generally, food trucks are self-sustaining, with pertinent equipment and supplies kept on board, whereas a food cart is a smaller operation, pulled behind a vehicle and reliant on a base kitchen for the heavier prep and storage. Both models can be found in many markets and are part of the mobile food-service industry.

This material provides expert insight and in-depth explanation of common steps toward starting a food truck business and its early days of creating its position in the market. Like most startup business books, this one defines a step-by-step process for creating a business plan, but this process is explained in a way that directly correlates to a mobile food business. Firsthand experience, interviews with subject matter experts, and personal anecdotes shared by other food truck owners are intertwined with the easy-to-follow explanation of how to start a food truck. Topics such as financing the business, creating a network of advisors, and filling each day with moments of joy are enhanced by the real stories and advice shared by a wide variety of people that comprise the food truck ecosystem.

Compare Business Models

Brick-and-mortar restaurants often require more financial risk and investment than food trucks command. It could be for that simple reason that brick-and-mortar establishments sometimes band together to push for regulation of food trucks to protect the market for standalone restaurants. That same reason may be why some municipalities tend to side with the brick-and-mortars rather than food trucks when zoning or ordinance issues come into question, since they appear to have longer commitment to a community as they cannot get up and move as easily. All forms of food-service business can be considered risky investments, but less financial risk on the part of an owner could suggest less financial commitment to a community. And certainly, the lower risk may be why food trucks are growing at a faster rate than brick-and-mortar restaurants.

Food trucks can be started with a startup cost of less than $100,000. That price tag is unlikely for a standalone restaurant. Additionally, food trucks are sometimes charging more than the nearby café for similar offerings. So why isn't the food truck concept taking over brick-and-mortar? The reasons are endless. Operating a food truck is not easy work. Imagine packing up your entire kitchen and service operation each day and starting nearly from scratch the next day. Or consider the seasonality of business due to weather. Or hear the stories firsthand from food truck operators who will tell of their average day starting at 4 a.m. and ending sometimes after 10 p.m. The life of a food truck owner-operator is not all fun and games. With appropriate business planning and management, a food truck can be profitable and often exciting.

Food trucks can be started with no long-term commitment. The cost of a food truck apparatus and equipment does not usually come near the cost of buildout and startup for a restaurant. If a location does not prove profitable for a food truck, it can be relocated often without additional cost. The break-even point also appears much earlier for a food truck due to lower startup and operating costs. A disadvantage of the food truck model over a restaurant is that the business operation may not be able to operate as efficiently, mostly because a food truck is having to handle product more often as they start or close for the day. Storage and space to organize inventory of supplies and equipment is also limited for food trucks when compared to brick-and-mortar restaurants, because of the reduced footprint. The ability to be mobile requires much planning and frequent moving of materials. The relationship with customers is also very different between the two business models. Customers can always find their favorite restaurant where they expect it to be, while food trucks, both to their advantage and disadvantage, often have less predictability of location for customers. In some cities, food trucks mirror brick-and-mortar businesses in that they stay planted in one location day after day, but more commonly, food trucks take advantage of their mobility. Austin, Texas is an example, though, of a food truck ecosystem that has been developed around the concept of food trucks that rent private property and only move once a year, for inspection and reviews.

Some businesses will choose to have both a restaurant

and a food truck so they can capitalize on the strengths of each model at various times. Commonly, a restaurant that owns a food truck will save on otherwise duplicated expenses of ordering, storage, and preparation space. Restaurants may also leverage the mobility of a food truck during festival season, when customers may not be visiting their brick-and-mortar as frequently—so the restaurants go to the customers instead of waiting out a down season or slow day. The strategy behind such an offering is like why many restaurants also provide catering services, and the difference is that their food truck is often in public-vending mode while their catering service is contracted by hosted events. Like a small franchise or chain, many efficiencies can be discovered by providing service from multiple locations.

As the lines continue to blur between indirect but competing industries, food-service providers are challenged to think outside the box and continuously vie for their share of the market(s). Quick-service restaurants (QSR), fine dining, food trucks, convenience-store food service, and ready meals at grocers are all options considered by the hungry diner. Then add in the delivery options that continue to explode from providers such as Amazon, Grubhub, and Instacart, to name a few. The conversation is often led by the battle for convenience and perceived value when trying to attract frequent customers, who could be worth exponentially more than the cost of their meal that day.

Food-Vending Apparatuses

This book uses the term *food truck* as a general term to encompass mobile kitchens or vending stations, which may be in the form of a food cart, frequently moved tent or vending apparatus, or a traditional food truck. However, the three models are different, and one may be preferred over another depending on the business goals and market opportunities.

A food cart is pulled behind a vehicle and usually dropped at a location for service. Food carts are notoriously smaller than food trucks, with many ranging from forty-five to seventy square feet. Some municipalities will limit the size of a food cart to sixty square feet or another size that is predetermined to meet their zoning needs. Food carts typically have limited warming and cooling equipment on board and are intended for food-service shifts of four hours or less. Food trucks may be more limited by municipalities or space restrictions regarding where they can serve but often are better equipped to provide storage, cooking, and service for several days before returning to base. Food trucks are their own vehicles and do not require additional vehicles to pull them but are also at the mercy of their own operation. Meanwhile, a food cart could be pulled by an alternative vehicle if necessary. Vending tents or hand-pulled carts require a vehicle to move them long distances and are frequently seen at large events or densely populated areas of commerce. Since both require less financial investment, they could provide a temporary startup solution for aspiring food-cart or food truck owners. Similarly, a food-truck or cart owner may also have equipment such as tents, chafing dishes, hand carts, or other equipment that may allow them to leave their larger, or sometimes more restricting, apparatus and serve from open air during an event. All mobile-vending operations need proper licensing and often permits or permission to vend at a desired location.

Some mobile food vendors will start small, to minimize their startup costs and investment risk, with the intent to grow into a larger and more versatile concept. Since a push cart or tent has very little investment for equipment, that could be a good start for someone who is limited on access to capital or time to manage and operate the business. From there, profits or credit could be used to upgrade the equipment to a cart or even a truck. An additional perk of starting small is that a customer base is already created, a menu refined, and stakeholder relationships developed before anyone invests in the larger operation. An additional risk of starting with smaller equipment and footprint is that the business may be less efficient or become accustomed to a brand and value that does not allow for the seamless growth.

*Photo Courtesy of: Meghan Blake-Horst, Food Cart
Parklet on 6th St. Austin, TX, January 2018.*

Lean Startup

A microbusiness such as a food truck is often synony-
mous with *lean startup*. The methodology of Lean Startup,
as developed by Eric Ries, receives criticism from some,
mostly when used by large corporations or when inter-
preted that a company should create average products for
average people. At the core of Lean Startup is the need
to build, measure, and learn. Since food trucks are often
started from scratch, without much of a blueprint, it is
crucial that the business can measure results and then
pivot quickly if needed. It is also possible, though not
always suggested, to start a food truck in forty-five days
with less than a $50,000 investment, which demonstrates
how it presents a minimum viable product (MVP). And
while some companies may measure success by volume of

units produced or by the bottom-line profit, a food truck often measures its early success by considering validated learning in its early years. MVP does not mean a product is of undesirable value but rather than it meets market needs and can likely be modified to continue growing in value after inception.

A major advantage of a lean startup is that the entrepreneur can stay solely focused on taking a very simple product to market, knowing that the product and the entire business can continue to morph and grow as learning occurs. Unlike the process of creating a complex organization that happens to produce or represent a series of products, food trucks can be as simple and straightforward as the owner is comfortable with. At its core, a food truck produces food products and sells it where the customer is. After opening the doors for business, a food truck entrepreneur may realize ways to improve the menu, location, or service. That process of continuous listening and learning may also uncover opportunities, such as additional revenue streams from creating value-added retail products, that were not realized during the creation of a business plan.

Insight: Rodeo Wagon

As the founder and owner of The Rodeo Wagon, I managed a lean start-up and found it a valuable process for entering a market with minimal investment before realizing revenue. I had zero experience managing a retail food operation, so I hired someone with that experience to help me create the business and evaluate it for feasibility before deciding to startup the business. Like the other businesses I have started, the food cart was inspired by identifying a need in the market and satisfying a personal thirst of learning to succeed in a space that was familiar but not comfortable for me. Plus, I love to be surrounded by delicious food and create experiences for people.

Food trucks are growing in popularity and do not require as large a financial risk as many other food-service businesses that someone could start. During the planning stage of the business, I considered the real possibility that I could realize the business was not going to be a good investment for me, so I was constantly evaluating the plan for its value as an investment, knowing that opening day may never arrive if I decided to pull the plug rather than pull the trigger.

Since the business model and funding process was rather simple in comparison to the more complex businesses I had started, I gave the research and planning process thirty days before a decision had to be made to either move toward opening day or simply chalk it up to a learning experience. By Day Twenty-Five, I had gathered enough information, analyzed the market, and planned the business startup enough to feel confident with a decision, so I decided to pull the trigger and jump into rapid development. By Day Forty-Five, The Rodeo Wagon was open for business and taking on a large public event for its first-day operation—that day was full of lessons and proof that a strong network of people who are willing to help is crucial!

A food truck does not produce revenue until it is open for business, so drawing out the planning process only delays the generation of revenue while depleting startup capital. No matter how much more planning could have been done, lessons would still be learned by the act of operating such a micro retail business. We adjusted the menu to be more efficient when procuring supplies, focused on the products that would sell, and used time trials to improve service time. We refined the process of selecting locations, which meant saying no to some opportunities to allow for others. And we had to grow a reputation to command the locations and shifts that were most profitable.

While learning to operate a food cart sustainably, hosted catering and broker food contracts became an additional stream of revenue. Eventually, a decision was made to focus on one or the other, since there was not staff and management capacity to do both, and so Rodeo Wagon halted food truck service to focus solely on catering and food-contract services. Starting as a food cart allowed for rather safe growth in customer base, experiences, vendor relationships, and staff.

Looking back, I am appreciative of staff, partners, and customers who helped the food cart find its position in the market. Those collaborations created the opportunity that later arose and allowed me to keep my eyes wide open to adapt as needed. Managing the cash flow was essential for the tiny business. Diversity in financing through loans, grants, and then liquidation of business assets, such as the food cart apparatus made it possible to safely invest in growth. Life as a food-cart owner is not always easy but can be rewarding in so many ways. And it certainly taught me to expect the unexpected. My advice for a new food truck owner would be to plan for the worst and hope for the best, but don't forget to find joy in the learning process.

Planning is important, but not more important than the execution of the plan. A plan that sits on the shelf is merely a hobby project or a means to an entirely different end. Perhaps most important for a food truck startup is to do enough planning to avoid unnecessary costs and risks but to open the doors as soon as feasibly possible. No matter how much time is spent on the plan, it will inevitably change once the business is operating, customers are providing feedback, and the entrepreneur is having those moments of realization that must be heard to pivot the business toward profitability.

Plan the Plan

When working toward a goal such as the startup of a food truck, it helps to have a plan in place that identifies the difference between planning and execution phases. SMART goals help the designer of a business to stay on track to opening day. Such goal setting can be helpful throughout various phases of business

planning and management. A SMART goal, as originally introduced by George Doran, Arthur Miller, and
James Cunningham, is specific, measurable, attainable,
relevant, and time-based. Partners can especially benefit from setting assignable and specific goals to avoid
duplicating efforts and keep the truck moving forward,
but solo entrepreneurs also benefit from the goal-set-
ting process. Unless they have accountability partners or
advisory teams in place to keep them on track, it is easy
for food truck entrepreneurs to get lost in a process or
distracted by less relevant details.

Chapter Two

The Food Truck Entrepreneur

Entrepreneurs are creators. They may be viewed by some as spontaneous risk-takers who are chasing a dream of avoiding the ladder climb that much of the civilized world suffers through, calluses and all. Perhaps that is because TV commercials and social media memes depict an image of twenty-somethings working from their couches or in co-working spaces surrounded by dozens of techies. It is an image that comes easily to mind when hearing the term *entrepreneur*. For most entrepreneurs, that description does not fit. Anyone can start a food truck. To clarify: not everyone should, but anyone is welcome to. The faces of food truck entrepreneurs, when filling a room, represent the diversity of the country. A variety of ages, races, and socio-economic statuses are included in the picture of food truck owners, and that drives this magical comradery that most operators share, where everyone is welcome at the table. Behind the scenes, in that space of shade behind the food trucks, owners share tales of the unexplainable and dine on each other's fare—after all, we all enjoy when someone else cooks for us, and the best compliment comes from another chef!

Webster's Dictionary defines an entrepreneur as one who organizes, manages, and assumes the risks of a business or enterprise. Investopedia expands on that by defining an entrepreneur as an individual who founds and runs a small business while assuming all the risks and rewards of the venture, rather than working as an employee. The entrepreneur is commonly seen as an innovator, a source of new ideas, goods, services and business/or procedures. That does not require the person to be spontaneous or to take risk without careful consideration of costs versus benefits or the break-even point of their venture. Rather, many entrepreneurs enjoy the art of finding alternative solutions and calculating (and recalculating in many cases) the outcomes when changing the variables. A better way of defining that seeming desire for risk may be to consider that an entrepreneur knows what they are willing to part with when seeking a value or outcome.

The definition of an entrepreneur also calls for the organization of a business. That means the entrepreneur is either creating or overseeing the startup process. That process could include identifying the idea, evaluating it, and validating it. The startup process often includes developing a business plan, identifying supply-and-distribution chains, working with key influencers, and crunching the numbers in projections. The entrepreneur is responsible for creating a company, from registering the entity, through the planning process, through the creation of necessary components and systems, and through its initial launch, when it generates that dollar bill that can be hung behind a register—or transferred electronically in many cases now. The definition of an entrepreneur does not require that one operates the business into the future or is even connected to the business after its conception.

Commonly, an entrepreneur will work on or in a business well after the business is launched, and many owners of young companies will still consider themselves entrepreneurs. Perhaps that is because young companies sometimes require so much pivoting and revision that the role of entrepreneur continues. After such time, an entrepreneur still in the position of ownership could simply be referred to as a business owner.

Finding an entrepreneur who did not take a financial risk when starting a business would be as difficult as finding an entrepreneur who did not have a vision. While some startups are funded by one person, others are funded by various sources that still include an investment by the person driving the bus. Whether an investment succeeded or failed at churning a profit, there was consideration of the cost and desired benefit. Anyone can become an entrepreneur, but the title is not for the faint of heart. According to The Kauffman Index 2017, each age group of 20–34, 35–44, 45–54, and 55–64 represents approximately a quarter of new entrepreneurs. Although the youngest age group represents the greatest span of years, it is not comprised of the greatest number of entrepreneurs. Immigrant entrepreneurs accounted for over 30 percent of new entrepreneurs.[10] The face of entrepreneurship is inclusive, so don't be surprised when you walk past a group of food trucks to find there are various ages and ethnicities looking back at you.

---

10 Fairlie, Robert, Arnobio Morelix, and Inara Tareque. "2017 Kauffman Index of Startup Activity." Kauffman Indicators of Entrepreneurship. May 2017. Accessed May 22, 2019. https://www.kauffman.org/kauffman-index/reporting/~/media/c9831094536646528ab012dcbd1f83be.ashx.

Meghan Blake-Horst, Street Vending Coordinator for City of Madison, Wisconsin, recognizes that it's mainly women and minorities who approach her with aspirations of starting a food cart or food truck. Many prospective cart owners are first-time business owners and new entrepreneurs, with combined motivations to either create self-employment opportunities or create jobs. Like many communities, her city is experiencing a seemingly continuous increase in the number of inquiries for starting a mobile vending business.

The motivations and limitations vary between entrepreneurs who are starting mobile food-vending businesses. There is a wide array of experience and education levels paired with sometimes drastically different visions of what success means for such a business. While one startup may plan for record-breaking sales out of the gates, many food truck entrepreneurs prepare for the sort of profits that could free them from employee roles while modestly providing income for their families. Depending on their skills and personality, some people may be able to take a do-it-yourself approach to the startup process, while others create a network of support that also consists of mentors, volunteers, vendors, and consultants to create their vision. Ultimately, it is important for entrepreneurs to self-assess their skills and expectations before determining how much help they will need to start a food truck.

Entrepreneurship is solidified when the business opens or the product goes to market. But the process begins before that moment. The process that led to the creation of a business often started as an idea. A soon-to-be entrepreneur may have seen a food truck that operated with many inefficiencies and wondered how to make it better. A soon-to-be food truck entrepreneur may have tasted a mouthwatering new dish and wondered if it could be the new trend of foodies. Or another entrepreneur may have seen worms on the ground after a rainstorm and considered how that seemingly free inventory could be monetized in a sustainable way. The inspiration can come from various sources. When screening ideas, here are a few considerations:

1. What is the product or solution your idea produced?

   Tip: Perhaps you have the best meatloaf recipe or your chili just won a local award, which inspired a desire to sell your chili to many other people.

2. At its core, what is behind your product?

   Tip: This is when you consider the technical aspect of your product. For a food truck, it may be the fact that it is a food business on wheels that can serve chili at the edge of a lake covered with people ice-fishing. Consider what benefit the product delivers.

3. Is the concept or the product innovative, or how is it unique?

   Tip: Of course, it is unique in some way, but is it unique enough that the average person will observe a difference?

4.   Does it solve a problem and for whom?

Tip: A person with a headache is possibly the easiest person to sell Tylenol to. What headache does your product solve?

5.   Who would pay money for access to the product?

Tip: Your mother does not count. Who would buy food from your food truck, and how can you best describe them? Consider demographics and psychographics. Some brands will go as far as creating an avatar so they keep their eyes on who the customer is.

6.   What is the value of your product?

Tip: More information will be uncovered through market research, but even in an early discovery phase, most entrepreneurs have a ballpark number in mind. How much is your product going to sell for? And for fun: how many units do you need to sell for that number to matter? This topic is better covered after researching the market, but again, most entrepreneurs consider this line of questions before going to the work of creating a business plan and spending resources on actual research.

7.   How big is the market for your product?

Tip: What is the market size, and how much share of the market could you reasonably go after?

8. What significant changes can you anticipate that would affect your product's value?

Tip: An analysis of strengths, weaknesses, opportunities, and threats (SWOT) may shed more light on this, but there may be some already-known factors that could be anticipated. For instance, regulations and ordinances are often a concern in the world of food trucks.

Identify Skills and Traits

Starting a business requires keen focus and purpose. There is a level of commitment required of entrepreneurs to pour their energy, and often dollars, into the planning and startup process. This requires constraint and dedication to staying the course. Many lenders and investors will acknowledge that they invest in the person as much as the business. That means that the skills and traits of the entrepreneur or leadership will be important to the value of a startup business. The person(s) who operates the business in its early stage will also set the culture and course of the business.

People who lack some of the skills needed to start a business may have enough drive and resourcefulness to still make it happen. The key to navigating, then, is to recognize weaknesses and fill them. To provide that diverse skill set to the backbone of a business, the entrepreneur

should recognize when help is needed. These are some of
the self-reflection questions to ask before getting too far
into the planning process of starting a food truck:

- Do I have experience starting a business?
- Am I capable of conducting and analyzing research?
- Do I have experience creating financial projections
  and interpreting financial reports?
- Do I have experience in the food-service industry or
  a similar service?
- Am I comfortable producing a business plan?
- What is the timeline for deciding if this is the right
  business for me to start?
- And what is the timeline for opening the business if
  I decide to?
- What are my concerns with starting the business?
- What are my weaknesses?
- My strengths?
- Who can I ask to help me with starting the business?
- Who will I call if I have a question during the
  startup process?
- How comfortable am I when navigating unknown
  territory?
- What do I do when faced with an obstacle?
- What task am I fearing most?
- How strong is my personal financial statement?
- Or how can I improve my personal finances, which
  will affect my ability to acquire startup funds?
- What is my threshold for risk?
- What am I willing to give up to achieve my goal?
- And what exactly is my goal?

- Do I know how to define and create my product?
- Am I comfortable with the skills and tools needed to market my product?
- Who are the five most important people required to form my business?
- What are my five unique skills or traits that make me think I would be a good entrepreneur?
- How strong are my personal relationships?
- How will I manage the stress of creating a business?
- Am I comfortable driving and maneuvering the food truck?
- How do I handle failure or rejection?

That list of questions could be seemingly endless, but it will remain that—just a list—until readers use it to really evaluate their purpose and shortcomings. A firm understanding of oneself is important to planning and setting realistic expectations. Businesses fail all the time. And as some thought leaders may imply, value is found when growing past a failure to realize the intended purpose. Naturally, most organizations are not started by someone intending to discover failure. By recognizing the potential threats and weaknesses, a successful entrepreneur can create networks or processes for minimizing the risk. Likewise, a person can also expand on their strengths and drive with such strengths while outsourcing the weaknesses or discomforts. Starting a business is not about overcoming weaknesses and becoming better at something that was a struggle. It often requires allowing strengths to shine and knowing when to hire someone better at the areas of weakness or energy-drains.

Entrepreneurs Don't Have to Do It All

Entrepreneurship does not require superhuman powers or for someone to be a Jack of all trades. Rather than stressing over what you do not know well, focus on what you do better than others. It is acceptable, and often advisable, to hire out your weaknesses and lean on others' strengths. Entrepreneurs are solution-finders.

Honesty is a building bock in the art of finding sanity when starting up a business. It is important to objectively evaluate what you are willing and able to do. A beauty of owning a business is that you do not have a boss who will review your resume and scrutinize your abilities or performance. However, that is because your abilities and willingness to persevere will ultimately determine your fate naturally. It is harmful to pretend skill sets are present when they are not. Likewise, it is not helpful for a night owl to think they will open a breakfast business without a drastic lifestyle change.

As an entrepreneur and business owner, you will not have a manager to correct your bad behavior or praise your milestones and accomplishments. If there are skills or personality traits that seem to be lacking in what is needed to create and operate a food truck business, there are options to overcome those obstacles. One option is pursuing education and training to improve your strength in those areas. Pursuit of self-improvement may reap the best results when there is marginal improvement needed either for skill or confidence in the skill. When there is a significant gap between an identified skill or trait needed for a venture, many people hire it out. It is common for a microbusiness owner to have contractors or vendors who perform tasks such as bookkeeping, consulting, marketing, or administrative work.

When business owners outsource time- or energy-consuming tasks core to keeping the business functioning, they often split their time between working in the business and working on the business. If owners outsource or hire the core production or service of the business while they work on the management and administrative functions, they are working on the business. Conversely, if the owners are solopreneurs performing all tasks related to producing and selling the product, while outsourcing the business function, they are working in the business. Commonly heard in mastermind groups, strategic-planning meetings, and business-coaching sessions is the question, "Do you spend the majority of your time working in the business or on the business?" Some may argue that the owner should work on the business while others recognize that the nature of a microbusiness may require an artisan of juggling: someone who can be a chameleon and wear the various hats while outsourcing only specific tasks. Ultimately, it depends on the specific business and person. Living outside the comfort zone is normal and expected of entrepreneurs but living in misery is not necessary. If you're miserable performing a function or simply don't have the ability, then there is no harm in asking for help. Just be sure to budget for it.

Some entrepreneurs consider themselves unemployable and will usually wear that badge with honor. It is not because they are unproductive or cannot show up on time; it is usually because they dance to their own tune.

If that is the case, they should learn how to listen to that tune as it may help them to be a genuine leader. There has already been an Anthony Bourdain, Jeff Bezos, and Pablo Picasso, but that is not who will create your food truck or be the best leader of your business. Entrepreneurs are creators, and the best thing they may create is the process that keeps their business moving forward despite their personal distractions or limitations.

Thanos Lemonidis, owner of the Gyros King Food Truck in Denver, Colorado, stated that the thing he would have done differently when starting the business, if he had known what he knows now, would be to make it a slow and steady expansion. Gyros King opened in 2017. It is building its third truck and looking to expand into the Arizona market in the winter.

Insight: Gyro King

Thanos Lemonidis, owner of the Gyros King Food Truck in Denver, Colorado, stated that the thing he would have done differently when starting the business, if he had known what he knows now, would be to make it a slow and steady expansion. Gyros King opened in 2017. It is building its third truck and looking to expand into the Arizona market in the winter.

Photo Courtesy of: Gyro King, Colorado, retrieved 2019.

An Average Day

Walking into a bone-chilling below-zero-degree freezer at 5 a.m. and answering the last email at 11 p.m. is not uncommon for a food truck owner. Joining the masses of people with carpal tunnel is not uncommon for entrepreneurs who are researching their startup dreams and cranking out pages of planning documents. Neither the startup nor operation processes of a food truck are for the faint of heart. Now if that did not scare anyone away, there is a silver lining in both the startup and operation of a food truck; the trick is finding it.

There will be days full of excitement and joy when self-proclaimed food critics scream from the rooftops of their social-media accounts about the accolades a food truck chef deserves. And there will be days when everything just fits in a perfect flow. Those days are what keep operators coming back for more—the moments when magic happens and you can provide the ultimate customer experience while the cash register rings faster than it ever has. It can be exhilarating and make all the work seem purposeful again.

When planning a business startup, there is often much excitement for the vision and even the journey of starting something new. Think back to other moments in life when the anticipation of something new was enough to prevent sleepless nights but not feel exhausted, because that adrenaline rush was better than the strongest cup of joe. Moving to a new city, starting a new career, having a baby; none were easy or lacked effort, but each likely came with its moments of revelation and excitement for the unknown. Creating a business from scratch will serve up that same dose of energy in the beginning. And then it gets real. Reverse and repeat. This is the roller coaster of entrepreneurship, and only the daring will avoid the eject button at the scariest moments.

For some people, the planning process can be condensed to a short forty-five-day window, while others may take a year to bring their food truck to market. Either route is still likely a lean startup with minimal financial risk (compared to bricks-and-mortar) but many moving parts. Anything longer than year may raise the question of whether the process was being taken seriously or if the potential entrepreneur got sucked into the black hole of planning. Starting a small business produces only expense and no revenue until the first sale is made. Why do some entrepreneurs seem to rush through the startup process?

The reason may simply be that it limits the time of feeding the money pit and jumpstarts the journey of moving the cash flow into a positive report. For others, they may expedite the startup process because they recognize that they wear special lenses that catch the glimmer of shiny objects, so they want to keep their energy hyper-focused until they cross the finish line of startup planning. And others may argue that they limit their planning time because they recognize that despite all the planning in the world, the first weeks or months of operation will be more enlightening than any book or report they discovered during the research process.

Describing an average day of the planning process is challenging because no two days are exactly alike, and that unpredictability does not change after the doors open. Creating a timeline and outline for the startup process can help keep everything moving forward rather than allowing a fine detail to command too much focus. Research, creation, and feedback would be three categories of activity that seem to appear on most days of the planning process.

While researching a topic within the business plan, the entrepreneur may be able to create product designs, financial documents, or other key pieces to the ultimate plan. While producing the plan, it is important to interact with people, for several reasons. First, we don't know what we don't know. Further revelations may be discovered—or at least any assumptions may be identified—by talking through a process or a finding with someone who has experience on the topic. Another reason for constant discussion with subject-matter experts (SME), is that it builds a natural network of support around the new business. People like to help people, so why not bring some SMEs along for the journey? And perhaps most importantly, working through findings and planning with other people can add a sense of realness to the process. It is easy to get caught up in the what-ifs and the grandiose visions of market domination when parental pride sets in for a business that is being created. It is also easy to get bored or frustrated with the mountains of paperwork and planning that go into starting a food truck, if all you want to do is serve good food and see a line of smiling diners in front of your truck— which of course will be in a premium location.

Creating a lifestyle that is conducive to getting a business off the ground can mean something different for each person. Setting aside specific blocks of time for planning the business will help keep the process on track. Some people are most productive working alone, from home. Others may need to find a co-working space or at least a coffee shop to absorb energy from the environment. Most people would benefit from always carrying a notebook (digital or paper) during the planning process, because inspiration can strike at the most unexpected moment. Keeping all notes and working documents in one place can help with organization and redundancy of work. There could be manic moments of inspiration during the process, which can lead to more extreme leaps in productivity; run with them. Keeping a flexible schedule with activities that compete for time and attention during the planning process frees up the ability to work when most productive. Trying to start a business on an already over-demanding schedule can be challenging and frustrating.

Not everyone quits their job, retires, or stops attending all social events before starting to plan their business. A bare calendar is not a requirement of success. However, lightening the load of commitments may be helpful during both planning and startup.

Photo Courtesy of: Thony Clarke, Mango Man, Madison, WI, Retrieved 2019.

Insight: Café Costa Rica

An average day of operating a food truck during its early months is vastly different than the startup planning process. Thony Clarke, owner and operator of Café Costa Rica, shares that his day often starts at 5:00 a.m. and he does not return home sometimes until 11:00 p.m. His schedule may vary from that of another food-cart operator, but he credits the long hours with his ability to decrease wait time for his customers and keep his cost of goods sold (COGS) in check. He makes a list every night before retiring to bed, so he can free his mind and start the morning fresh, even before his mind wants to function again.

Arriving early, with a list in hand, allows him to pull the appropriate fixings from the walk-in cooler and freezer when he arrives to the shared kitchen, which functions as his base kitchen. He then prepares for lunch shift, to be out the door by 9:00 a.m. Why so early? His customer base can be found waiting for him to open at 11:00 a.m., so he wants to get parked by 9:30 a.m. to be greeting customers by 10:45 a.m. After parking, there is still much to do that could not be avoided by prep time at the kitchen. Generators must be turned on, cookware must warm, and the supplies in the cart must be organized differently than they were for transport.

Customers do not want to wait more than two minutes for their food, so preparing for efficient service is key to keeping happy customers during a service shift. Practice also helps shave the service time. As a single operator on the cart, Chef Thony continues to work on efficiency while being careful not to sacrifice quality of product or service. He can now serve fifteen people in ten minutes. That is up to 270 people during a lunch shift that operates 11:00 a.m.– 2:00 p.m. That is more people than many restaurants serve during lunch in the same area. And that is why so much preparation and planning is required. Not every day results in a maximum-capacity production run. A dreary, rainy day may keep the food cart parked at its base kitchen or send him packing after moments of service and hours of preparation.

Food trucks in general do not want to run out of food, though, since every dollar and every customer moves it closer to becoming profitable or growing the income.

Café Costa Rica is not new to the market, but Chef Thony continues to think of ways he can be innovative. Since opening, his menu and operational plan have changed. He created additional revenue streams by starting retail lines of products, including sauces and chips that he sells to other food vendors and through grocers. Those additional streams of revenue may induce extra-long hours during peak seasons but also help supplement his income during off seasons or periods of time when the weather prevents traditional food truck service.

Traditionally, lunch shifts end around 2:00 p.m., so there are opportunities for a food truck to still serve dinner or late night in the same day, and that is where the late hours come from. Some trucks will opt to serve breakfast and then lunch rather than staying out until later in the day. It is common for a solopreneur to operate their food truck for seven to ten service shifts per week. Trucks with additional staff operate closer to fifteen to twenty shifts per week if they can find the right staff and locations to fill the schedule. Consider that overhead of the business is usually around 30 percent of the expense, but further efficiencies can be found if the variables of COGS and labor may increase while overhead stays constant. For many food truck owners, the cost of their apparatus or vehicle is their largest overhead expense, followed by equipment on the truck. The cost of the apparatus and equipment does not change (usually) if the truck serves twice as many customers as usual. After a dinner or late-night shift, the truck operator is tired but must find the energy to load out, clean up, and plan for tomorrow. Some trucks will hire someone specifically for that load-out or dish-cleaning process since the operator's energy and even safety could be questionable by that point in the day.

Time Out

Before working through the intense process of starting a food truck business from scratch, entrepreneurs should self-assess their motivations and limitations while considering if this is the lifestyle they want. There is nothing wrong with walking away from an idea for a business, even when the planning is nearing completion. Not every business idea was meant to be started as a business. Not every person finds benefit over cost when starting or running a business. It is less costly to walk today than tomorrow, and that almost always holds true, at any point of starting up or running a business that is not (yet) profitable.

During the planning process, entrepreneurs may realize that the business they envisioned is not the best fit for the market or for their motivations. But that business concept, or some of the work that went into it, may be useful for another type of business, so less is lost by terminating the plan. Sometimes, during the planning process it becomes evident that, with a pivot, there is something solid to the business. That same eye for the pivot is valuable when operating a small business. When obstacles or threats present themselves to a business, they can often be viewed as opportunities if spun in the right direction. Knowing when to open that valve and let the energy flow though is an artform.

Another common reaction to the realization of how much work is involved in starting a small business from scratch is to buy into a franchise or purchase the blueprints of a business. Either route can save a business owner time and resources compared to creating everything from scratch, and many studies show that franchises have a better chance of survival or success. And it is okay if some decide they do not want to create a business from scratch. While they are not entrepreneurs at that point, they are still business owners. Starting a business can be rewarding for various reasons, but it is not for everyone.

Chapter Three

Legal and Regulations

Mobile food-vending businesses reside in a space that requires acute attention to legal and licensing matters. While the regulations continue to change in many markets, there are usually permits and licensing specific to mobile food vending. Before obtaining such permits to conduct business, standard legal matters must be addressed to form and protect the business. It can be overwhelming to manage the legal needs of a food truck, but it is crucial to protecting the business and its shareholder(s).

Insight: Street-Vending Coordinator

Meghan Blake-Horst is a street-vending coordinator. Her position exists within the Department of Economic Development. As the previous owner of several small-business ventures, she empathizes with the current and aspiring entrepreneurs whom she works with. Regulations surrounding mobile food vendors are complex and made more confusing by the language used by the various governing bodies.

She suggests that anyone planning to start a food

truck business speak with their local vending coordinator, or someone in a similar position, before spending a dime on any equipment. Too often, she encounters people who purchased a full apparatus or some equipment for their business before realizing the limitations they may be creating by doing so. In her community, there are size restrictions on each type of vending operation. If a business's apparatus does not meet the requirements or the generator is too loud, she cannot grant a permit to vend in the city. For cities that do not have a vending coordinator, businesses can start by asking the city clerk's office who to speak with, since that is usually the office where they will purchase their permit for vending.

She also suggests speaking with the local health inspector to understand requirements that must be met before a food truck can obtain a license. Basically, the Department of Health provides the license to operate as a retail food business, and the city provides the permit to sell the products in that area. Both are necessary. For startups that are entering the space by acquiring a food truck from someone who is currently operating it, realize that permits and licenses are not always transferrable and may need to be replaced before the new owner operates the business.

Food trucks must keep up with the changing regulations in the area(s) they vend. Noncompliance can lead to warnings, fines, or the termination of permits. Keep in mind that a general permit in a municipality may not be the same permit needed for vending in high-density locations, special events, or other designated areas that require additional permits.

Meghan communicates with various stakeholders of the food truck ecosystem throughout the country and acknowledges that any two markets can be dramatically different from each other in how they regulate the industry. Some cities are more welcoming than others, and yet a commonality is that many are struggling to catch up their response to the growth of mobile food vending. Regardless of which community a food truck plans to operate in, she stresses the importance of asking a lot of questions often.

Permits and Licenses

Mobile food vendors are required to hold licenses and permits beyond those typically associated with a brick-and-mortar retail or food business, though local, county, and state government requirements may vary from one area to another. A food truck owner should plan for a base license, mobile retail or restaurant license, and a vending permit or license, in addition to any others mandated by governing bodies in the area they prepare or serve food. Commonly, food trucks may hold permits from several communities they serve. More broadly, there is usually a need for a general business license, service-establishment permit, and food-safety license. Some licenses may require testing or proof of other credentials, such as a ServSafe Manager certificate, while others require the completion of a form and payment to process the license. Festivals or other special events may require additional permits aside from those mandated to regular service providers in that municipality. And many private and public governing bodies will require proof of insurance, while some will also require indemnification or being listed on the food trucks insurance as an additional insured entity, which can be displayed on a Certificate of Insurance (COI).

Some municipalities may welcome and encourage food trucks, while others may regulate to minimize growth in the industry. Regardless, it is helpful to understand that there can be benefits to regulations if they are reasonable, understandable, and enforceable. Such regulations may protect severity of volatility in the market as related to changes in zoning, regulations, or other permissions. After a 2008 study conducted by researchers at Portland State University, which found significant benefits to the citizens by having food trucks present, the city of Portland encouraged food truck clusters, referred to as "pods," to occupy vacant property. Food Carts Portland now estimates the city has more than five hundred mobile food vendors. While the population of Portland is smaller than Chicago, Portland far surpasses its larger counterpart with the number of food trucks, since only seventy licensed food trucks operate in Chicago.[11]

---

11 "America's Food-Truck Industry is Growing Rapidly Despite Roadblocks." The Economist. May 4, 2017. Accessed April 12, 2019. https://www.economist.com/graphic-detail/2017/05/04/americas-food-truck-industry-is-growing-rapidly-despite-roadblocks.

Vehicle

Whether you have a food truck or cart, there must be a vehicle for transporting the business, and that vehicle will need to be licensed through the Department of Motor Vehicles. Many states also require that the vehicle be insured. Depending on the size of the vehicle, it may require a special driver's license to operate it. Knowing the weight of the vehicle and all equipment either on it or behind it will be important because of restrictions for traveling on certain roads. Also, the driver will need to know the height and weight of the entire apparatus since that may limit where it can travel. Considerations can also be taken regarding fuel economy and how much torque a vehicle may need to easily navigate with the additional weight.

Food Handler's Permit

Some cities and states require one or more employees of a food truck to get a food handler's permit. The governing body may require one or more employees to take a food-safety class before the permit is issued. While some municipalities require that someone with a certification be present during operation, others may just require that the person(s) with food safety certification be regularly employed by the business. When in doubt, ask questions of the health department that governs the area of service.

Department of Health License

Just as any restaurant is required to be inspected by the health department, your food truck (and commissary) will also need to be inspected prior to opening. Many counties or states will require two licenses: one for the base kitchen and one for the mobile retail apparatus. The review and approval of your local health department will verify that the food you prepare is being maintained and created in a safe manner. Such permits often need to be renewed annually and may require additional inspections while in operation. Health departments usually have the authority to fine or document a business that is operating out of compliance. Some food trucks apply for a state license so they can conduct business in multiple counties, while others may stay specific to one county and therefore apply for the county-level license. Health departments will commonly require the following categories be addressed and will publish specific requirements of each, so it is important to check with local inspectors before building the apparatus.

Water:

- Gravity or pressurized water-storage tank that provides hot and cold water under pressure and is constructed of specified material or another durable food-grade material.
- Specific tank capacity for mobile food establishments that serve beverages or food or reheat prepared foods to allow for employee handwashing.

- The water tanks must have a gauge that allows the operator to see the amount of water in the tank.

Other:

- Return to its service base not less than the mandated intervals for servicing and maintenance.
- Have equipment that is commercial grade.
- Have adequate non-hand-operated handwashing facilities supplied with soap and single use toweling.
- Have adequate ventilation and fire-extinguishing equipment.
- Have a properly air-gapped, commercial-grade food-preparation sink, if food preparation is occurring on the unit.
- Have smooth, non-absorbent, and easy-to-clean surfaces.
- Have commercial-approved utensil-washing facilities if not conducted at the service base.

Applicants should be prepared to answer questions and demonstrate the operational plan, which often needs to be submitted in writing as well, when the inspector is considering licensing the operation. The operational plan should include a diagram of the layout and flow of operation.

Vending Permit

Even with the appropriate health licenses, many communities and events will require a vending permit. Contacting the city clerk's office is an appropriate place to start when inquiring of vending permits that may needed within that city.

Fire Certificates

In some markets and at many special events, the fire department will inspect your food truck if you are using cooking equipment on board. They will educate you on the regulations you need to follow and do routine inspections on your food truck fire-suppression system. Some of the basic requirements will include having a safe method for trapping grease and having more than one fire extinguisher within reach.

Seller's Permit

Obtain a state seller's permit number through the state's department of revenue. This is required as part of most license applications. The seller's permit will allow a retail business to purchase wholesale goods intended for resale without paying sales tax. The permit will also require the retailer to report all sales revenue and pay the appropriate sales taxes on a regular basis—usually monthly or quarterly. To gain a seller's permit, most states require the business to have an EIN provided by the federal government.

Employer Identification Number

It is free to obtain an Employer Identification Number (EIN), which can be obtained through the Internal

Revenue Service at IRS.gov. Businesses that operate as a partnership or corporation, or have employees, are required to have an EIN. Many businesses that are not required to have an EIN will still acquire one since that identification is often required when opening a bank account, applying for a loan, or obtaining a retail license. It is also common for suppliers and vendors to require an EIN since that is tied to the business's credit rating.

Certificate of Insurance

Many cities now require insurance before a food cart may operate within the city limits. The requirement is like working with private events. A challenge for carts is that very few carriers will provide general coverage for such a business. Events and catering opportunities may also require a rider or listing of additional insured. Auto insurance, general liability insurance, and workers' compensation are the primary insurance coverages needed. It is not uncommon for an event or city to demand $1 million in coverage. Note that audits happen regularly, and it is important to comply since they may result in credits or decreased costs as time goes on, whereas failure to comply can result in termination or penalty fees. Also, remember not to overestimate revenue or payroll when applying for insurance, since that will result in additional premiums.

Why Regulations Are on the Rise

The growth in popularity of food trucks, coupled with the public perception and concern for safety, results in some of

the changes of this increasingly regulated space in which
food trucks reside. There are still populations who view
street fare as unhealthy fast food, though many of the new-
est trucks are combating the perception by serving local,
fresh fare. Alliances and single restaurants are raising questions to protect their market, which is sometimes threatened by food trucks serving near their stores. And some
municipalities simply do not have accurate or enough policies in place to properly regulate the current food truck
scene. For all those reasons, mobile food vendors are having
to keep a close eye on changes to regulations.

There is a lot of cross-pollination of competition now
that convenience stores (C-stores), quick service restaurants (QSRs), fast food, and food trucks are all competing
for a similar customer. Convenience stores are increasingly
offering grab-and-go dining options, a step up from their
traditional roller dogs and cold ready sandwiches. Quick-
service restaurants shook up the restaurant scene for the
past two decades, and now their space is being shared by
food trucks. Fast food was confronted by the trends of
healthier eating and felt the loss, so they can be especially
threatened by the entrance of new food trucks, which
also often aim to get their customers past their window
in under two minutes. There is no question that dining
options are multiplying. If it were not for the increased
spending on convenience services in the US, the food-service industry would be further cannibalizing itself.

There is a lack of national standards for street vending,
and many trucks are operating without proper licensing.
The mobility of food trucks and the pop-up store environment they create make them difficult to regulate in many

cities. In cities such as Los Angeles and New York, there is a high demand for street food, but licensing costs are also high enough to deter some vendors from going through the proper licensing channels. New York City grants three thousand permits annually for selling food from trucks or carts. And still, the lengthy waitlist means that an operator may wait up to ten years to legally be licensed. Those who choose not to wait are rolling the dice and operating without licenses. Despite its challenges, the mobile food-service industry continues to thrive. Establishments that carry unique local style and offer healthy alternatives and relative affordability are often the ones that succeed.

Mission: Food Safety

Imagine the crisis that could unfold from the lack of practicing food safety. Someone could be harmed by chemical, biological, physical, or sanitary hazards, and the business may need to enact a crisis-management plan. Most communities with mobile food-vending regulations require someone on staff to be certified as a manager through ServSafe or a similar food-safety program. Some opportunities available to a food truck may require that all staff have training and certification for the safe handling of food. During the business-planning process, a food truck entrepreneur can account for training costs and time. Safety equipment and best practices should also be budgeted for during the operation of a food truck. Note that requirements may vary by market. For instance, the operation pictured below, from Crash Boat Beach in Aguadilla, Puerto Rico, is a common setup to be found on the beaches of Puerto Rico. The vendor is a recognized icon of the beach as it serves delicious local fare to a steady line of regular customers, fishermen, and tourists. However, their operation may not meet regulations in an area that has steeper regulations or enforcement of operational layouts. It is important to balance the fabrication and layout designs to accommodate expectations of local customers while meeting all area regulations.

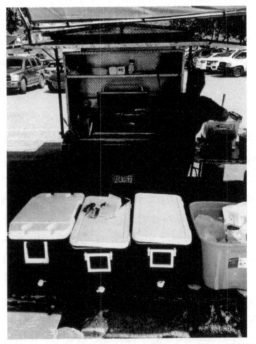

Photo Source: Kay-Tee Olds, Aguadilla, Puerto Rico, 2017.

Before food is ever touched by a food truck owner or staff member, there are safety precautions to take. Safe sourcing of products can protect the business and its customers. Health inspectors may prefer a food truck to source through food distributors with good reputations for food safety. The food is often tracked, transported at appropriate temperatures, and properly stored immediately upon arrival at a delivery point. The concern is legitimate when considering that some food trucks will transport food from suppliers on their own, in vehicles that do not have regulated temperatures. That may not appear to be a problem if the temperature outside is not within the danger zone of 41 to 135 degrees, but the reality is that the weather is not that predictable in most areas. Then there are concerns with sanitation and handling. When possible, food truck owners will coordinate delivery of their food supplies in a way that constantly monitors and protects the food against growth of pathogens or other health concerns. That can be especially challenging when trying to source small batch or hyper-local perishables. Having an insulated Cambro or similar piece of equipment makes it possible to transport foods that are sensitive to time and temperature.

Personal hygiene may seem to be a personal issue that business leaders may hesitate to address with employees of other industries. However, this is a food-service business, and that means food safety plays a role in nearly every activity and decision. A correctly set-up handwashing sink on a food truck or at an event should have water that can free-flow once started and should be stocked with hand soap and one-use paper towels or an air dryer. There should be a garbage can for debris and a gray water bucket or tank to catch waste water. Luxuries such as lotions and antiseptics are welcome but not necessary. Since single-use gloves, handwashing supplies, hair nets or hats, aprons, and handwashing equipment will be used continuously, they should also be budgeted for on a continuous basis, which can be reflected in cash-flow projections. After that expense, it would be unfortunate if an employee's actions were to create an environment of food-safety hazard, so training and performance evaluations should also be part of the continuous operation plan.

Having the proper equipment and enough small wares accessible during prep or service will make life easier and can lead to a safer environment for customers and employees. Since it would not be a safety best practice to use the same cutting board for raw meat as you would for raw vegetables, food trucks will need more than one cutting board. The same thought process would apply to so many items on a food truck that a business plan and cash-flow projection should allow for multiples of many small wares and tools. Items such as thermometers, which play a big role in the well-known need for controlling time and temperature to protect food, seem to grow feet and walk away from a kitchen or food truck, so stocking up on multiple could be warranted.

Local food and health agencies that regulate the area where food-truck employees handle food have their own set of rules that a food-truck business must comply with. For instance, some agencies may require three or four sinks to be on board for proper sanitation. Some may require wing faucets, and others may require all equipment to be certified by the National Sanitation Foundation (NSF). And some agencies will require all employees, contractors, or volunteers to complete a health-reporting form. Meeting with a local health inspector before purchasing equipment and finalizing the operational plan, can save time and money during the startup process.

Business Formation

Registering a business with the state's department of revenue is not an overly complicated process. In fact, it is often faster and easier than applying for any of the required licenses that are unique to operating a food truck. Before registering a business, consider what type of business it will be and who will own all or part of it. Not all businesses need to be registered federally, but most retail business owners will do so, even if they do not have employees, so they can receive a tax-exempt status when purchasing from wholesalers.

Business Registration

In most states, business owners are required to register their business with a state tax agency and apply for certain tax permits as a seller. You may need to apply for a state sales tax permit. If you plan to hire employees, you also need an Employer Identification Number (EIN), which will be your federal tax ID. Your federal tax ID is used when you file tax returns. It is used in place of your personal Social Security number (SSN) when you need to show business identification, thus keeping your SSN protected from public eyes when business documents are published. Even if you are not hiring employees, you will need an EIN if you are incorporated (as a C corporation, LLC, etc.).

Types of Legal Business Entities

General Partnership—This type of entity requires multiple partners who own and operate the business. This is a common business type for food trucks that have more than one owner. Every partner in a general partnership is responsible for the business and is subject to unlimited liability for business debts.

Limited Liability Company—A Limited Liability Company (LLC) can be formed by an individual, more than one individual, or entities that have a special written agreement. The agreement details the organization of the LLC, including provisions for management, assignability of interests, and distribution of profits and losses. The primary incentive for creating an LLC is to avoid personal liability for the debts of a business. Only the LLC is liable for the debts and liabilities incurred by the business—not the owners or managers, *IF* personal guarantees are not signed with vendors and personal monies are not mingled. This may be the most common entity type for food trucks since many are individually owned.

Limited Partnerships—A Limited Partnership (LLP) provides for one or more general partners and one or more limited partners. The general partners manage the business and share fully in its profits and losses. Limited partners share in the profits of the business, but their losses are limited to the extent of their investment. Limited partners do not usually participate in the day-to-day operations of the business

C Corporations— A C corporation may continue to exist after removal of the founder or owner because it is a separate entity than the individual. Rather the organization is owned by shareholders. A board of directors is responsible for making key decisions and overseeing policies. Profits are reported under schedule C on taxes and reported to the State Attorney General. This would not be a common form of entity for a food truck.

S Corporations—S corporations and C corporations have similarities, but S corps are only required to file taxes annually. Taxes are reported on personal returns as the profits are passed down to the shareholders. S corporations, like C corporations allow for investors, liability protection, and life after the exit of a founder. It would be rare for food trucks to identify as this entity type.

Single-Member Limited Liability Companies (SMLLC)— This is an LLC owned by a single individual and the title declares that without further inspection who the member(s) are, which is the difference between an SMLLC and an LLC. This would be a common entity type for food trucks.

Personal Service Corporations (PSC)—This type of entity is formed to provide a personal service. To be a PSC, the owner must perform at least twenty percent of the services themselves and own at least ten percent of the business on the final day of the initial test year. This would not be a common entity type for a food truck.

Entity Types in Review

LLC is a unique business type that can provide significant liability protection to individuals, and it is available in most states. It limits liability if you play by the rules, and it can be very easy to set up. Two important factors to keep in mind when protecting liability: don't mix funds and beware that personal guarantees will override the liability protection. When considering starting the business alone or as a partnership, consider your capacity for risk and comfort in sharing. It may seem simple to partner with someone but remember that we all have different drivers and the dynamics will inevitably change over time. If you set up a partnership, be sure that roles and expectations are clear and that you have established a plan for solving differences in goals or operation in the future. Also, determine buyout or exit options. Partnerships can be a way of having more skills within the corporation and limiting cash outlay during startup, but some owners may be best-suited for hiring out their weaknesses rather than sharing equity.

Operating Agreements for Partners

With more than one person making decisions and affecting outcomes, various aspects of starting and running the business need to be addressed up front. Certain entities also require an operating agreement as a part of the incorporation articles. This agreement details the business ownership and responsibilities of partners. The clearer and more complete the agreement, the less that is up for debate or disagreement when dilemmas arise.

The operating agreements should address contributions, distributions, defining ownership, decision making, and dispute resolution. They should clearly outline how much each person is contributing to the business during startup and if additional funds are needed in the future. The agreements should also clearly explain when and how distributions will happen so there is no confusion and less friction over the topic as partners look to realize profits or repayments from the business. Aside from the basic definition of who owns what percent of the business, and that portion of profit and liability, it should define what happens at the onset of unplanned-for variables such as death, marriage, divorce, long-term or terminal illness, or bankruptcy. Partners can avoid unnecessary friction and keep the business moving forward by clearly separating tasks or decision-making responsibilities. Yet there should still be a plan in writing to determine how disputes will be handled. And to protect the business from a partner leaving, setting up a new company, and stealing the customers, a non-compete clause should be in place. Finally, the dissolution process of the partnership should be predetermined before the partnership starts operating a business. What happens if someone wants to sell or exit? What happens if an offer to purchase the business happens before the exit plan called for such a move? Basically, the operating agreement should define who is doing what, who is responsible or has rights to what, and how unplanned events should be handled.

Chapter Four

Marketing

Data, physical elements, event logistics, and even a recipe for that soon-to-be-world-famous street fare can be manipulated with great predictably. People are another story. Customers, employees, and collaborators require ongoing attention and can be the cause of much frustration if a business does not set clear expectations and react consistently. Conversely, people can be the largest asset of a business when everyone is on the same page and the symbolic bus filled with such people has everyone moving in the same direction.

Marketing at a Glance

At its core, marketing is the act of promoting and selling a product in a way that maximizes its impact or profit. An audience must know of your product and how it meets a need or interest of theirs. Marketing principles also play a role in determining price and place of a product, so it can be accessible to the target audience. The education about what a product's purpose is or how it works is part of the marketing efforts.

Small businesses with equally small budgets may be intimidated by the large budgets and resources that arm large brands. However, locally owned independent businesses also have an advantage of being able to be directly in front of their customers, in person. Today's customers may value convenience or experience over pricing, so it does not always have to be a price war between big and small. Grass-roots marketing still has power in the marketplace; the tools of delivery just continue to change.

Advertising is possibly the most popular type of marketing, and many people will confuse the difference. It is part of marketing, but just part of it. The art of marketing is broader than advertising and sales promotions. Marketing can be seen in the development of a brand, packaging of a product, and creation of educational materials. Advertising is the creation and delivery of content to your audience in a way that educates or influences them in favor of your product or initiative. Every interaction with a customer involves marketing—or potentially the lack of marketing. After getting a customer to your location or product, marketing efforts continue through the engagement process. The experience a customer has with the environment around a product, staff at the retail location, and the product itself is all part of the value a food truck is providing. Imagine if a business invested in branding itself, producing appealing packaging, and generating a mouth-watering menu, but then failed to train staff to engage in a consistent manner with customers. The cycle of marketing would be broken. Food trucks have a potential advantage in that they can interact directly with the customer while the product is being ordered and often during the start of the product consumption. Applying customer feedback to future processes can help the business to define its unique selling proposition and create a competitive advantage.

The need for marketing does not stop when the doors open; rather, it continues to grow in importance. Marketing is an ongoing process that demands attention. A marketing strategy can help grow a business through attraction of customers and then sustain the customer base while continuing to strengthen retention. Some food truck owners avoid the cash outlay of hiring a marketing manager or firm by tackling the marketing efforts on their own. The risk that small retail-business owners could face when handling their own marketing is the distraction from other priorities and often the lack of consistency because their attention is pulled in several directions.

Consider the difference between strategy and tactics. It is important to understand and plan for both. Some would argue that it is more important to make one person's day magical than it is to be seen by a hundred people. That is because the interaction becomes memorable and leaves a lasting impression, which can influence that person's future purchasing and recommendations.

Loyalty programs have steadily grown in popularity and become common among retailers who want to drive more frequent and larger purchases from their customer base. Reaching the right customer is only the first step. Once you've acquired new followers, it is important to keep the connection strong. One study, published by Harvard Business Review, discovered that a business' profit could be increased by twenty-five to ninety-five percent by increasing retention rates by five percent. That fact becomes more impressive when considering that acquisition cost of a new customer can be five to twenty-five times more than the cost of retaining a customer. [12] Several point-of-sale (POS) systems provide loyalty marketing solutions that are integrated so the process of connecting with customers on a regular basis is not so cumbersome. Various forms of loyalty marketing can be observed when visiting food trucks. Some trucks use paper punch cards, others integrate within their POS, and others focus on social-media followers to drive loyalty metrics. Ultimately, it should cost less to keep a customer than gain a customer, so many retailers will reward loyalty to increase revenue without being reliant solely on gaining new customers. With the volatility of sales from one day to another, for a food truck that parks in a location for a regular dinner shift, visits from loyal customers can ease the pain on a bad-weather or slow-traffic day, when the market size in that area is diminished.

Food truck operators become busy in the day-to-day activity of operating their business. They must consider who is going to manage communication with customers and prospects. That person(s) should be able and willing to communicate with prospects in a timely and professional manner. A common complaint from coordinators who work with food trucks is their lack of response or lack of follow-through. Simply having a person designated to respond to inquiries, quote services, and follow up with

---

12 Gallo, Amy. "The Value of Keeping the Right Customers." Harvard Business Review. November 05, 2014. Accessed March 22, 2019. https://hbr.org/2014/10/the-value-of-keeping-the-right-customers.

those opportunities could provide a unique advantage to a food truck. Similarly, food truck operators often get busy working on other aspects of the business and forget, or do not make time, to manage their brand on social media and to publicly answer questions or comments about or to them. Poor reviews especially demand a response. Sometimes a seemingly negative interaction triggered by a customer on social media can lead to an unplanned opportunity to talk about values of the business or receive support from other customers. When reacting to a negative or combative message, it is crucial that the person representing the food truck is objective, calm, and looking to spin the conversation in a way that leaves each party with a better sense of value.

Ten Food Truck Marketing Hacks

1. Start Early: Secrets are harmful, and that is certainly the case for a startup business that will need a following once the doors are open. Tell everyone about your business and start growing the following of supporters well before the doors open.

2. Create Brand Ambassadors: Personal selling can be powerful, but there simply are not enough hours in a day for a business owner to talk one on one with every prospective customer. Multiply that effort by encouraging your biggest fans to tell your story, share pictures of your tasty dishes, and invite their network of people to jump on the bandwagon.

3. Remember That Marketing Touches Everything: No rock should be left unturned. There are opportunities to promote the brand or build its value around every corner. Remember that even a chance conversation with a stranger may affect their perception of your business. And poor driving skills while hauling your branded trailer or truck could prove wrong the saying that "no PR is bad PR."

4. Create a Content Calendar: Having a plan will keep you on track with driving the message forward. There may be products, specials, or locations to be promoted. Be sure that all forms of communication are accounted for, including social media calendars, e-blasts, message boards on the truck, etc. All vehicles of communication should be integrated and speaking the same language.

5. Automate: This is especially helpful for the busy days or the days that are just plain tough. Marketing automation may include the use of software to connect efforts involving social media, email marketing, live chats on your website, and feedback forms.

6. Stickers: They are simple to procure and inexpensive yet valuable tools that can be used in so many ways. Handing them out to kiddos may prompt their parents to become a customer. They can be placed on packaging so that your customers are walking billboards for the brand, and they can be

placed on marketing material that may be printed black and white but needs that pop of color.

7. Own Your Brand: Everything a customer interacts with should reinforce the brand. From the design of the menu and apparatus to the greeting, customers receive and the persona that is portrayed on social media, everything should reinforce the mission, vision, and values of the brand as a continuation of the customer experience.

8. Park to Advertise: A well-branded food truck can act as a highly visible billboard when it is parked in strategic locations while displaying promotional messaging. Rather than parking behind a building or in a low-traffic neighborhood overnight, some food truck owners decide to park their moving bill-boards on main throughways or near their service locations, so they are advertising tools even when not in use. Many food trucks design their apparatus to advertise their menu or like the image, promote other services such as catering. For instance, the Memphis-based food truck pictured below, pro-motes their catering services, with verbiage next to their service window.

Kay-Tee Olds, Memphis, TN, March 2019.

9. Respond to Everything: Make a goal to respond to every customer within a business hour. This can increase bookings and de-escalate complaints. Some small businesses hire out the direct communication since it tends to peak during the same hours as dinner service. It makes sense: more customers reach out to a business during or shortly after an interaction with it.

10. Listen: Even silence can be an important message to receive. Read the body language of customers, hear their feedback about their experience, and listen to what is happening in the market. Understanding the customer's perception of the business and recognizing opportunities to strengthen the value of the brand are essential to refining the message, product, and brand. Change is inevitable, and it's

important to keep eyes and ears wide open to know when a change should happen.

Marketing Cycle

Various descriptions of a marketing cycle can be described, but ultimately it is a process of research, goals, execution, and analysis. Within each step of the cycle, subsets of the category can be defined. For instance, within execution, there would be stages of creating materials, determining a distribution channel, and delivering a message or promotion. Each business may approach their marketing from a different angle, and that can help each business remains unique from others.

Thorough market research should be conducted before any other step in the marketing process. During this stage, assumptions should either be justified by sound facts or discarded. For a well-organized research process, a startup can define a problem or hypothesis, then design a research plan, gather a credible amount of data, and then analyze the findings. After those steps, decisions can be made that are supported by sound research. Consider that decisions made of assumptions or inaccurate data can lead to missed opportunities or wasted resources, and they can cause business owners to potentially miss the mark entirely when creating a marketing plan that will drive sustainable business growth. Just because a flock of food trucks jockeys for a location does not mean that location is the most profitable opportunity. Research can help overcome the barriers of assumptions.

Only after research is conducted and analyzed will an

entrepreneur be able to accurately define market opportunities with certainty and be able to determine reasonable goals. Strategic goals should be obtainable and measurable. Marketing goals, like other wisely planned goals, should be specific, measurable, achievable, relevant, and within a determined time frame. The goals of a small business should align with the market and the personal goals of the business owner. Unlike a large publicly traded corporation, independent business owners can work a business plan that leads to the exit plan predetermined by that owner. In some cases, lifestyle may be the most important factor, and so a food truck owner may select a location that supports their goal of working certain days of the week or months of the year. If you know you are not a morning person, breakfast shift may not be the best fit, for instance. Or similarly, if complex event planning creates extreme anxiety, then regular lunch shifts may be a better fit than large multi-day events. Available service times should be part of the research process and marketing efforts in general. Similarly, the financial projections and business should reflect such goals.

During the execution stage of a marketing cycle, a business will produce materials, policies, and procedures that convey the brand and supporting information that came out of the research and goal setting. This is also the stage when communication with the customer happens. Food trucks are not limited to signage, social media, and packaging to convey their message. However, those tend to be significant communication tools for a food truck. After creating a brand, the business owners should eat, breathe, and live it in everything they do. Consider the brand disconnect that could happen if a go-green brand were to advertise heavily in print mediums. Or the irony of a taco-themed food truck using pizza boxes or serving Italian pasta dishes. Or any food truck not using visuals to promote their food.

Evaluation of marketing results should happen regularly through an analysis of the marketing cycle, to determine which marketing activities were effective and how effective they were. The marketing cycle is different than the market cycle, which looks at the cycles an entire market goes through rather than an individual company or product. Analysis of a company's marketing achievements can be best measured if appropriate and measurable goals were set. Return on investment is a common target for businesses that are determining if their investment in marketing, advertising, and sales initiatives produced a net gain. Whatever the benchmarks were, it is important to evaluate the performance of a marketing cycle objectively, since that analysis will lead into the next round of research, goal setting, and execution. Using inaccurate data or justifying performance with excuses is a good way to set a business up for future failures and misguided goals. It would be better to determine the failure of an effort and correct it for the next cycle. Failures and mistakes happen, but loss can be minimized if lessons are learned and corrections are applied. Food truck owners often take personal pride in the performance and perception of their business. If owners cannot objectively evaluate the marketing results, then they should involve a third party to do so. If the business owners have an advisory board or informal network of advisors, they can go to their subject-matter experts to provide that objective analysis.

Marketing Principles

The marketing mix is comprised of product, place (distribution), promotion, and pricing strategies. The Four P's should be considered during the planning, implementation, and evaluation of any marketing cycle. The principles of marketing are also crucial elements to define within the marketing section of a business plan, which may be used internally as a navigation tool or while meeting with future investors or lenders. When evaluating a marketing effort that is focused on one segment of the Four P's, it is important to consider how it could affect the performance of the other principles.

Product

Product often drives the conversation for entrepreneurs, while marketers may come from another angle. Frequently, an entrepreneur who is starting a food truck may have the product already visualized before researching much about the market opportunities and threats. It is okay to be inspired first by product, if the product has its place in the market and can command enough demand to create a sustainable business. The product's physical and emotional attributes should both be considered since customers often buy for emotional reasons rather than features of a product. The business could consider how their product will look, feel, smell, and satisfy the customer. And remember that a weakened place, price, or promotion may overwhelm even the best-planned product.

Place

The consideration of place includes more than the physical location of a retail store. Food-truck owners must consider the location of their food truck during service and while parked. Marketing value can be found during off times if the truck is parked strategically and captures the attention of passersby. Supply-and-distribution channels are also part of the place principle, since the supplies that go into making a product can affect its viability, and so can the ability to distribute the product. For food truck businesses, the supply channel can have a negative effect on their product and distribution if a distributor fails to make delivery on time or changes vendors of a supply. In the end, the location of a food truck during service hours is the most important place element to plan and will have the greatest effect on profitability regarding place factors.

Consider cost versus benefit when determining if a certain location or channel is worth the investment. Just because there is high foot traffic at a location does not mean that the cost related to it will be offset and produce the greatest profit. Some premium locations come with permit or event fees. A break-even analysis can help evaluate if the place is worth the investment or if a location with fewer sales but less cost would be more profitable in the moment—and toward the long-term value of a brand.

Promotion

Many people think of promotions naturally when thinking about marketing. While promotions are not the only

facet of marketing, they are certainly a crucial part of the
marketing mix. The promotions mix is a subset of marketing that includes public relations, advertising, sales
promotion, and direct selling. Startups should consider
their business goals, which were derived from a combination of research and personal motivations or limitations,
when determining their promotional efforts. While creating promotions, remember there is a difference between
how customers connect emotionally with the promotion
of a feature and how they connect with a benefit. Well-
executed promotions will leave customers with visions
of the benefits they will receive from the product. Too
often, businesses cut their promotion budgets to save the
bottom line but that is a short-term solution that creates
long-term repercussions. Startup businesses, that rely on
business-to-consumer (B2C) sales, should instead set
aside a larger budget to promote their business – consider
15% of revenue during launch months.

Advertising is communication through paid outlets, to
reach borrowed audiences. Print, radio, television, and
physical displays are examples of traditional mediums.
Modern mediums operate on the same premise of gaining attention of a borrowed audience but use digital or
mobile outlets to do so. Advertising can be especially
useful for introducing a new product or creating a new
customer base, since the advertisers can pay to have their
pre-recorded or designed ads in front of otherwise strangers to the business.

Public relations include earned media efforts and focuses
on the public image or reputation of a brand. Cause marketing, press releases, and interviews are common forms

of public relations efforts. When done correctly, public relations can lead to increased awareness and perception of a brand, product, or initiative. Food trucks may participate in fundraisers for goodwill or provide cooking demonstrations on a local TV show as part of their public relations strategy. The primary differences between public relations and advertising are the amount of control over the message a business has and the lack of guarantee that a message will be shared with a borrowed audience. An argument could be made that while there is more risk in getting return on investment from public relations, since coverage and message are not guaranteed or purchased, the value of such coverage could influence customers further than a paid advertisement could, primarily because it is perceived to be more natural and less salesy.

Sales promotions happen in-store or on-site. They commonly include demonstrations, signage, contests, and incentives. Common sales promotions include buy-one-get-one-free (BOGO) offers, tasting demonstrations of a product, and contests to participate in some way for the chance to win a prize. When holding a contest, caution should be taken that it does not require purchase or unreasonable participation, or it could become a lottery, which is regulated by different laws and fees. Sales promotions can be used to get an initial purchase from a customer, receive a large purchase from that customer, or encourage more frequent visits. Menu and signage on a food truck are part of sales promotions. When designing the menu and other regular signage that may need to be changed from one event to another, consider using templates or materials that can be modified without requiring the purchase of entirely new signage. Some food trucks use chalk boards or menu boards that hold removable pieces of material for the constant changes to menu items and pricing.

Personal selling is possibly the least efficient but most effective means of promotion to an individual. While communicating directly one on one with a customer has its advantages, since the pitch or promotion can be tailored and adjusted during the interaction, it would also be close to impossible to perform such a tactic with every potential customer in a market, due to the sheer time and personnel that it requires. Food truck operators naturally have a direct-marketing opportunity when a customer walks near their truck or comes up to the window considering ordering a meal.

Direct marketing is often confused with personal selling but does not require an ongoing two-way conversation. This form of promotional marketing can be seen when a customer receives ongoing personalized communication from a company that introduces new products that may interest that customer or that encourages further action from that person. For instance, a company may send out emails, text messages, or digital ads because of a person's previous activity. Consider how you start searching for something online and then seemingly magically start seeing ads all over your email and Facebook page for similar products. That is an example of direct marketing using current digital tools.

Sweat equity can help keep cash costs down as a small business when starting to market it. However, it is important to realize that time spent on saving marketing costs can also distract business owners from other core business-management functions and drain their energy before they can excel in their areas of strength. Identifying a budget for appropriate promotions of the brand will alleviate some stress and keep an accurate account of money needed to execute promotional strategies effectively and sustainably. Some food truck owners handle their own promotional efforts while others outsource this area. If solo entrepreneurs are handling their own marketing promotions, it will be important to use tools that provide efficiency. Mobile apps allow busy people to design ads or edit images, so a busy food truck owner can work remotely and produce timely content. There are also social-media and content-management systems that can be synced with multiple platforms, so the business owner can log into one site rather than half a dozen while working on the go. Another way to work efficiently with content creation is to have a graphic designer design templates so temporary menus, promotional cards, or ads can be created without having to start from scratch.

Content calendars can provide structure and keep food truck owners focused on their goals while communicating through social media, email, traditional media, or even in person on their trucks. A best practice could be to identify topics related to financial and marketing goals for each month or quarter and then identify strategies to achieve the related goals. If a business owner expected to launch a new sandwich product in July, then all the platforms could include content about that product, and the business owner could lead into such a launch by talking with customers and sharing related content leading up to that date, as demonstrated on the content calendar. Such a calendar can also keep social-media managers in a proactive role rather than reacting to shiny objects only.

Price

The value a person is willing to give up to obtain a product is the price that can be derived from a product. There are several pricing strategies a business can use when determining the price of a product. Profit-oriented pricing will maximize the profit margin of a product without necessarily considering such factors as the ability to sell complementary products or build a loyal following. Profit pricing primarily focuses on creating the greatest margin between the cost of the product and the price that a customer pays for it. Sale-oriented pricing focuses more on market share and being able to capture a larger percent of the market. Such pricing could mean more volatility for the business's pricing structure since the business may need to continually pivot while reacting to other key players in the market. Status-quo pricing may require the least attention to market shifts, as it prices a product at a rate that could be reasonably paid by the average consumer. Money is often left on the table, but the business can function with steady costs and revenues.

Many food trucks will price on what the market will bear (WTMWB) and will adjust their pricing at different venues depending on what competitor pricing is and what the customer views as perceived value. The lowest price a food truck should charge on a regular basis is that which is greater than the cost of goods, including variable labor costs related to that product. Arguably, the food truck should either have products with greater margins as well, to cover overhead, or another stream of revenue that does so. Ideally, the WTMWB pricing optimizes the revenue and profitability. A food truck that charges eight dollars for a meal, when the customer is willing to pay ten dollars, is leaving money on the table. However, if the food truck is charging that same customer twelve dollars, there is more consideration in the buying cycle and often less frequent sales or lower volume of sales, which can apply added pressure to each purchase to cover overhead and owner's draws. Also consider how sales tax is incorporated; since most food trucks in many markets do not add sales tax above the listed menu price, customers become shocked when it happens, and trucks are forced to carry a larger starting cash drawer to make such change. Sales tax can be built into the menu price listed.

SWOT Analysis

Strengths, weaknesses, opportunities, and threats are evaluated during a SWOT analysis. Most business plans will include such a report. Some businesses will continue to monitor SWOT as factors change throughout time, and many businesses will conduct a SWOT before launching or changing a product. Another purpose for conducting this form of analysis is to demonstrate market knowledge and highlight key points of interest for an investor or lender.

Strengths and weaknesses are often unique to the business or product that is being analyzed. By identifying the strengths and weaknesses of a product or business, the owner can apply that information when making strategic decisions. The analysis of strengths and weaknesses may also unveil unique selling propositions, which can be promoted or integrated within the marketing plan and execution. Weaknesses especially can be monitored and often counteracted with appropriate measures. For instance, food truck entrepreneurs who know their marketing collateral or financial records are weak can outsource the work or get training to help them produce a better result. Similarly, if a unique, custom-created sauce is a strength and in high demand by customers, a food truck business may decide to promote that sauce or even create an additional revenue stream by monetizing it through retail avenues. Objective evaluation is important when reviewing strengths and weaknesses, as they can only be capitalized on or protected against if they are first recognized.

Opportunities and threats are not unique to the business as they account for external or environmental factors. It is likely that several food truck owners in a market will identify similar opportunities and threats. The difference is how they work them to their advantage. Some may view one thing as an opportunity while others view it as a threat. Consider construction on a busy throughway nearby: that could be positive for one while negative for another. The growth of popularity for consuming animal-free or gluten-free products may help one food truck while harming another. Identifying such threats or opportunities early on can be beneficial since doing so allows a business to pivot as needed without rushing with reaction. Recognizing such factors during the planning stage of a food truck may also allow the entrepreneur to adjust the business offering or plan to capitalize on the opportunities and avoid the worst of the threats. Significant signs of threats may also be reason to pause or end a plan to open the food truck before it launches. Like food truck owners, investors and lenders will consider the damage or potential that a significant threat or opportunity may represent.

Target Markets

Planning for customers of a new business requires identifying target markets. Those could include varying levels such as primary, secondary, and tertiary markets. The primary target market represents the largest segment of customers. The market can be defined by demographics and psychographics. Factors such as their location, level of income, gender, ethnicity, dining habits, passions, and age, could be reasons they are part of a target market. After identifying a primary target market, a business can work the same process to determine secondary and then tertiary markets. Understanding who the customer is will make it easier to decide which type of advertising or communication styles and methodologies would be most effective.

Creating an Avatar

To keep the conversation about the people, some marketers create an avatar to represent a target market. They may create a collage of magazine clippings or design the avatar using computer software. The avatar is a character that can help the marketer or business owner remember who they are serving and who they are speaking with when making strategic decisions or creating content that represents the business. If the primary customer at the food truck's lunch location is likely a young, professional urban woman who is short on time but keen on finding vegetarian dishes, then the marketing efforts will be quite different than when catering to an older man who is price conscious and wants volume over health qualities. Whoever the most common customer is for a food truck in that location, an avatar can be constructed. Sometimes it is helpful to give that sample customer—the avatar—a name. If that avatar's name is Amy, for instance, it becomes easier and more natural to think, "What would Amy think of this new menu item?" or "How would Amy respond to this new loyalty program?" Marketing is most effective when the business manager remembers that it is still people that make the decisions. Each person is choosing whether to dine at the food truck today.

Chapter Five

Location, Location, Location

Place is a primary element of the marketing mix and could be the most important for a food truck. Unlike brick-and-mortar establishments, food trucks can go to the customer and change their location daily. Conversely, disadvantages of mobility are that customers may not always know where to find their favorite vendor or the sales on a given day could be sacrificed when trying various locations. Like any retail establishment, the location of a food truck plays a large role in how convenient it is for a customer.

Regulations of where and when a food truck may vend will greatly vary from one municipality to another and possibly from one year to another, mostly because of local government response to a rapidly growing industry that is demanding attention. Some municipalities have different rules for food carts versus food trucks, and some markets are the inverse of others. For instance, in Madison, Wisconsin, food carts with a total footprint of fifty-six feet or less may vend within the city limits by purchasing a vending license and holding the appropriate health and tax licenses, but there are additional restrictions within their downtown. Until 2018, food carts were only allowed to vend in the right of way, on public property, and business owners had to move the apparatus once the service shift ended. Carts are now able to also vend on private property with the appropriate permissions. In other cities, such as Austin, Texas, food trucks are commonly found on private property and immobile until their annual inspection, when they must move from their location to have their apparatus inspected.

In many markets where mobile food vending is allowed on private property, the property becomes monetized as it would be for rental of a brick-and-mortar space. However, in some markets, municipalities are inviting food trucks to use undeveloped land free of charge to fill a need within a food desert. It is important to ask questions often to avoid building a business around an assumption or temporary opportunity. Some mobile food vendors find it valuable to get involved with their local government, so they can advocate for their interests and know when zoning or other policies could change and influence their business model.

Foot traffic is not enough. When identifying locations for vending, a food truck owner should consider the brand and how it would be perceived by the audience in an area. If there are already three taco trucks on a city block, it may not be the best place to open another taco truck, unless there is enough demand for such cuisine in that area. If customers near a college campus are accustomed to buying three-dollar spring rolls for lunch, it may be because that is their budget, and so a BBQ truck selling twelve-dollar meals may struggle to sell the same volume as the spring-roll truck in that area. Just because one truck excels or struggles in an area does not mean the same will hold true for another truck. Creating a competitive advantage in the area or service and finding locations that have an audience that fits your demographic and psychographic target are all part of the art behind owning your brand.

When starting a food truck, it can be challenging to find the best locations. Consider location opportunities when designing a brand and menu, since they are all interconnected. Common areas for food trucks to be located are busy foot-traffic areas, business parks where food options are otherwise limited, late-night entertainment districts that are heavy on beverages and entertainment but light on food options, and events. There are also alliances of food trucks that will collaboratively target bedroom communities, which requires consistency and marketing to build a customer base that could support such an operation. While some communities let food trucks jockey for their location, other communities may have a method for regulating the placement of food trucks. If there is a system in place to determine which trucks get to park at certain locations, there may be rating systems or costs involved with acquiring such a desired location. When reviewing the following list, which is intended to spark ideas of where to do business, keep in mind that local regulations should be considered before acting.

Photo Courtesy of: Warren Hansen, State St. Mall Madison, WI, Spring 2014

Ten Places to Park a Frequently Moved Food Truck

1. Busy street corners

   This is a popular approach. It worked for Walgreens, right? Check with the city to understand if it is a first-come-first-served process for vending at a corner or if there is a process to determine which vendor(s) can park there.

2. Church parking lots

   Places of worship may welcome a food truck, to encourage fellowship or draw in the general public. Such a location could be best directly following a service. This may also provide opportunities for special gatherings hosted at the location.

3. Business parks

   Perfect lunch-service location. Hundreds or thousands of employees may have limited time for lunch and not many dining options that do not require them getting to their vehicles or leaving the premises. Consider creating a schedule and sticking to it so diners know which days they can find your truck at their location.

4. Bedroom communities

   Neighborhoods that are flush with homes but lacking retail and dining options are common especially in suburban areas. Like the concept of a business-park schedule, the same practice in a bedroom community can help create a larger customer base if neighbors know which days and times to expect a food truck in their area.

5. Park-and-ride lots

   This could be an option for trucks that also park somewhere else during lunch service, since the peak times would be during morning and evening commutes. Check local regulations. Vending may have to happen from the street or sidewalk rather than in the lot.

6. Big box stores on Black Friday

   Again, check with local zoning regulations, but if
   it is allowed, retail locations may welcome a partnership on their busiest days, if for no other reason
   than to keep their customers from being hangry.

7. Tailgate zones

   Be considerate of brick-and-mortar restaurants
   when pursuing this route. It may be best to park
   near lots or bars that do not sell food.

8. Breweries

   Distilleries and craft-beer breweries are popping up
   throughout the country, and many of them welcome the presence of a food truck with open arms
   since it keeps customers from having to leave their
   location to find food during their visit.

9. Schools

   Many cities have rules against vending within a
   certain proximity of a public school, but some still
   allow it. Otherwise, consider community colleges
   and universities.

10. Restaurant under construction

People already expect to be at this location for their lunch or dinner. Sometimes restaurants will encourage such an act to keep the traffic flow headed there during their down time. Businesses that have cafeterias under construction will also be receptive to the idea of helping them feed their hungry employees.

It is important to check with local regulations before planning to open for business in any of the locations suggested in this book as rules vary from one market to another. Some food truck operators prefer to be where the crowds already are while others prefer a location that is set apart from competitors. Either methodology can be advantageous, so it is essential to consider your brand and unique selling proposition before deciding what is right for your unique business. And always be conscious of where and when your target market will be ready to buy from your food truck.

Special-Event Planning

While some food-truck owners choose to serve from neighborhood corners or densely populated areas, where they can run on their own schedule and often be there on the dates of their choosing, others will work with events that can draw larger audiences or provide a control mechanism to balance the ratio of vendors to customers. Participating in a coordinated special event requires a greater commitment to a schedule and typically a larger upfront financial commitment. The reason many food-truck owners decide to take on the added responsibility and risk is because of the greater potential of revenue peaks. One well-planned and executed event can produce more revenue than a month of regular lunch service. However, the spike in revenue can come at a great risk and require a significant commitment of resources. Another option for participating in events is to work with smaller groups, which may offer crowds somewhere between a regular dinner shift and a larger event. During this section, consider events that rely on public purchases, and exclude hosted events that could be considered catered events.

Smaller public events may be hosted by local chambers, fundraising groups of nonprofits, or other event coordinators. A smaller event, for the sake of defining the difference in this section, may have one to five food vendors and under ten thousand attendees. Often the smaller events will be more flexible to work with but may also lack the structure or marketing power to command the volume of sales that a larger event can produce. It is becoming common for small events to look to food trucks as a source of revenue, so they will charge for admission and sometimes for a deposit, which can be earned back through following the terms of the agreement. The additional cost of the entrance fee can prevent food trucks from realizing a profit or increase their risk of experiencing a net loss on the event. To reduce the risk, food-truck owners can ask for references and speak with previous food vendors before committing to such an event. It is also common to negotiate the terms of a vendor fee, especially if the event runs the risk of unhappy sponsors or attendees if the food truck does not provide service. Commission fees, where the amount is dependent on the total revenue received, are not uncommon. Fees for passing an agreed-upon revenue amount is also a regular practice, in which food vendors only pay the space fee if they surpass a set amount of revenue that could be their break-even point. Small events are often more difficult to plan for logistically because of the variables and their potential for experiencing significant swing in outcomes. When planning for such an event, food-truck owners may prepare food for the minimum break-even point but transport enough food supplies for double the expectation, so they are not leaving money on the table if customer demand is greater than planned.

In this context, large events for independently owned food trucks have more than ten thousand attendees or a likely potential to produce greater than $10,000 in revenue for a food vendor. When planning to serve one thousand customers at an event, there is a different process for planning inventory, logistics, and risk control than there is at a smaller event or regular service shift. Menus can be balanced between products that are perishable and need special transportation or holding, and products that can be shelf-stable. Staff can also be staggered during the event, even with on-call staffing solutions in case demand is greater than planned. And money can be monitored and protected throughout the event to prevent loss through theft. Most large events will require a commission fee with deposit or a flat fee for participation. When planning cash flow, consider that event fees are often due months before revenue is generated at an event. The most profitable events may be the toughest to get into since previous vendors may not want to lose their spot—so new vendors wait either for someone to leave or be removed or for the event to expand its vendor slots. Plan the work and then work the plan for large events. There is no such thing as food vendors over-planning when venturing into a new large event, because their ability to manage the variables will greatly affect their ability to turn profit rather than risk a significant loss.

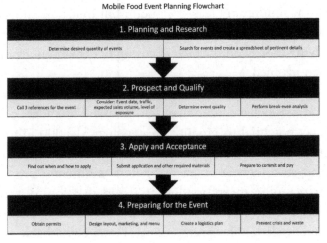

Chart Courtesy of: Mobile Contessa Media, 2018.

Research

The event-planning process starts with research and planning. After determining the number of events that would be manageable—and the size of those events—a food-truck owner can research a determined area for possible opportunities. Through speaking with event coordinators, looking online for events, and speaking with other food vendors, a list can be created. The list of opportunities should exceed the desired number of events that a food-truck business will work with, since they will likely not all pan out. When searching for event opportunities, it is important to keep a database, which could be as basic as an Excel spreadsheet, that houses the pertinent information. Event date, application date, contact information, location, and notes sections would be helpful for future reference. For focusing efforts, consider a column for prioritizing level of interest in each event.

Prospect and Qualify

After finding events through brainstorming, it is time to prospect and qualify the events to determine which opportunities may be best. Consider the date of each event and what other opportunities it may be competing with. An event on the Fourth of July may have more competition than an event on a random Sunday. If an event is on a key date, food trucks may want to consider the cost of saying no to other opportunities when weighing the value of the event. Then talk to previous vendors and look at social media and other media coverage that could shed light on past performance of the event. Some event coordinators will provide such contacts and links to coverage when asked. It could be cause for concern if an event coordinator will not release such supporting data to verify the validity of their event for food vendors. After gathering information about past performance, consider the type of menu that could perform well at the event and conduct a break-even analysis to determine how many units would need to be sold to produce the desired profit. Also consider the marketing value of an event. Sometimes an event may produce minimal profit on the day of event yet be likely to produce future opportunities or increase the reach of a food truck that needs exposure. Ultimately, food truck owners will need to decide what they need to receive from the event to make it a valuable investment.

Equation to find the number of units needed to reach a break-even point:

$$\left(\frac{\text{Total fixed costs of production}}{\text{Price per unit}} \right) - \text{Variable costs to produce the product}$$

Image Courtesy of: Mobile Contessa Media, 2019.

Application and Acceptance

After determining which events to pursue, it is time to apply for the event and build it into the cash-flow projection. It would be a best practice to determine the likelihood of securing the event and estimate the revenue and expenses by a percent of likelihood. This process is considered *pacing* in a sales environment. For instance, if there is a 50 percent chance of securing the event, that percent could be applied to revenue and expenses when budgeting the cash flow for that time. The application process can vary by event. Some will require upfront deposits before considering an application, so thorough research and analysis is important before applying. The application process may require submission of a menu, pictures of the apparatus or setup, references from other events or at least respected names in the industry, certificate of insurance, and copies of licenses and permits. Some may also require safety or operations plans while others may even require background checks or a list of employees who may be involved. Once accepted to an event, a food truck business will often be required to submit paperwork, logo, and marketing materials and sometimes to commit to cross-promoting the event. The time span between application and acceptance can be one week to six months. The application process often starts nearly a year before an event and almost always happens at least three months in advance of the event date.

Event Planning

After being accepted into the event as a food vendor, the logistics planning commences. Determining the menu for the event will dictate some of the equipment needs and layout, staff quantity and skill levels, and supplies. After creating the menu and deciding which equipment will be needed to operate effectively for the volume expected, it could be helpful to work with a food distributor to plan delivery of supplies. Some events will have freezer or cooler trucks on-site for vendors to use during a multi-day event. When there is not such a cooling truck on-site, it becomes even more important to plan for inventory to arrive in intervals, since space will be limited for storage in or near a food truck. Some food truck operations assign a staff person to be a runner, and that person goes back and forth either to a base kitchen or to the cooler trucks to replenish inventory on the truck as needed. Many food-truck businesses at events will expand their food truck with a tent to allow for more servers or storage and prep space. For the extremely busy events, most truck operators will plan a menu that requires minimal prep on-site and few steps in the serving process. Such menu items are often referred to as *scoop and serve*. By keeping inventory stocked appropriately, planning a menu for fast service, and creating an inviting layout, a food truck business can quickly multiply how many people it can serve per minute. Speeding up the process without sacrificing customer experience is key to maximizing profit in a business that thrives on managing the margins.

Planning for the unexpected occurrences is an oxymoron for food-truck owners, since one of the only predictable elements of food-truck operations is that the unexpected will become the norm. Having a crisis-management plan and posting it in a clear place for employees to reference it at an event could mean the difference between managing a potential crisis and being consumed by it. Also important is to plan for variances in volume or inventory. If sales are underwhelming, it can be comforting to know that additional shipments of product can be cancelled or at least saved to offset future costs. Perishables such as green salads may need to be donated if not used at an event, but unused packaging or frozen goods can be either returned to a distributor, if unopened and within policy, or saved for future events. A tip for managing the overabundance of inventory at an event that did not perform at expected levels is to change the menu for the remaining portion of the event, if event rules allow for changes, to move the perishable goods and take demand off the products that can be used for a future event or lunch shift.

Weather can cause great shifts in the tone and success of an event. It is an uncontrollable factor, but plans can be created to minimize its negative impact if the weather turns unruly. The same can be said about creating plans for capitalizing on the extremes. If the weather is untraditionally hot, and if the event allows for menu changes, a food-truck owner could add ice cream, sports drinks, or other cold treats to the menu while eliminating some of the heavier hot items. If the weather becomes dangerous due to storms or other threatening conditions, there should already be a plan in place for what to do and when. Sometimes it is worth losing a day of revenue to protect equipment, inventory, and staff. Consider how quickly an operation could be shut down in case of emergency. That consideration may affect the layout at an event or the type of equipment that is used.

Simply being at an event with a lot of people does not mean that each food truck will sell the same quantity as the vendor next to them or down the row. Location, menu, and appearance will determine who has the competitive advantage and who sells the most. Negotiating a prime location with the event coordinator may not be the easiest task for a vendor who is new to the event, but it is extremely important. Consider what unique value you bring to the event, and leverage that to gain a premium location that matches your brand. For instance, if you have kid-friendly menu items, jockey for locations near kid-friendly attractions. Someone who sells pretzel necklaces could request to be next to the beer tent. And someone who sells finger foods could be a good candidate for placement near the busiest music stage. Regardless of what food is being sold and where the tent or truck is set up, visibility is always key. Lights at night, an open view to food prep, and menus legible from a distance will invite passersby. Some events allow sampling, which means an employee could draw in crowds. Other events may allow non-food sales, such as koozies or rain gear. And rarely does it happen, but you may be able to have an ATM at your vending site, which could draw customers in at an event that provides limited access to cash. Similarly, allowing credit cards and promoting that option could be an advantage if other vendors are only accepting cash.

When preparing for an event, the food truck manager must consider all aspects of the event needs. Staffing, inventory, operation layout, transportation, cash flow, and backup plans for the inevitable upsets that will occur are all part of the planning process leading up to the execution of an event. The following checklist can be helpful when considering which events to participate in, planning for them, and enjoying the successes.

Event-Planning Checklist

I. Planning and Research

- **Determine the number of events you can handle for a designated period**
  Tip: Mark the number of days or weekends open for events on a calendar

- **Search for events and record pertinent information for consideration**
  Tip: It is unlikely that every prospected event will come to fruition, so triple the quantity when creating a list of prospects.
  - Name of event
  - Date(s)
  - Website address
  - Contact information (try to find a person instead of a generic email address)
  - Application deadline
  - Your level of interest in this event (scale of 1-10)

II. Prospect and Qualify

- **Gather three references for the event**
  Tip: Many food-truck owners skip this step, but it may be the best way to reduce risk. Ask the previous food vendors about traffic flow, prime locations at the event, average price of food at the event, peak versus low times. If it is a multi-day event, ask about the logistics of storing food in freezer trucks or being

able to access the vending location daily with a truck or handcart. Especially ask what the biggest challenge is when working at this event.

- **Consider logistics:**
  Tip: The following factors are crucial to determining the feasibility of an event
  - Event date
  - Event traffic
  - Expected sales volume
  - Level of exposure

- **Determine event quality**
  Tip: Find out which other food vendors will be at the event, and investigate their quality, theme, and price points.

- **Perform break-even analysis**
  Tip: Number of units sold to break even = Fixed costs / (Sales price per unit–Variable cost per unit). Fixed costs do not change pending quantity. Sales price is per unit. Variable costs will change pending volume.

III. Apply and Acceptance

- **Prepare professional materials**
  Tip: This means typing the application and proofreading thoroughly. If this is not a strength, then ask someone to review it. Forgetting to complete a section may be immediate cause for rejection.

- **Submit application and other required materials**
  Tip: Make sure the food truck's business website and social pages are updated, since event organizers may look there. Be sure to link to visuals or provide them in low-resolution format—it is annoying to receive anything over 2 MB in an email.

- **Prepare to commit and pay**
  Tip: Setting aside funds for the deposit and/or entrance fee will make it easier to react when the event produces a contract that must be turned around quickly.

IV. Preparing for the Event

- **Make license and permit arrangements**
  Tip: If you don't have a state license, you may need to get a local daily license. You may also need to pay an inspection fee to the event's operating city or county unless otherwise arranged. Some states require a vending license at events, while some municipalities offer a process for the event to procure the temporary restaurant licenses and schedule inspections.

- **Design equipment layout**
  Tip: Adopt an open and welcoming appearance and create a line flow that can efficiently handle overcapacity.

- **Develop event menu**

- **Devise marketing plan to maximize event sales**
  Tip: Many food vendors will rely on the event organizer to market the event, but they will have better sales if they also market the event.

- **Design, produce, and distribute signage and other marketing materials**
  Tip: Outsource marketing planning and implementation to increase efficiency and effectiveness.

- **Run time trials**
  Tip: Practice the preparation of a dish and running the register to determine how long it takes to move a person through the service line.

- **Check with food distributor about delivering to the event**
  Tip: Sometimes a distributor will have a cooler truck on-site. If so, set up an account and ask to keep key ingredients stocked in case you need them. This also allows you to stock less in advance.

- **Determine lodging needs and establish overnight travel policies**
  Tip: Some event coordinators will provide a list of lodging options and some may provide on-site lodging for a fee. Vacation rental sites are also an option in many cities.

- **Develop a crisis-management plan for anticipated customer or staff emergencies**

Tip: Post the plan clearly for operators and provide backup contact information.

- **Plan for unused inventory**
  Tip: With consideration for the tired staff at the end of the event, what should they do with the extra inventory if it's more than what you normally store?

- **Complete as much prep work as possible before the event**
  Tip: Inevitably, there will be unexpected circumstances or timely needs that arise during the setup and service operations at an event site so the more preparation that can be done in advance will allow key personnel to address the pressing issues calmly.

Beyond the Event

Part of the appeal to vend at large events, aside from the potential of greater revenue, is the marketing value. However, unless a food truck is well-equipped to capture customer data, or it excels in another form of marketing, it is rare for customers to recall where they ate at an event. To combat that, some food truck businesses use their POS to capture the contact information of customers, so they can reach them in the future with additional marketing materials. Others may promote social-media engagement at the event so diners are driven to their social-media page to post photos and reviews or simply start following the truck on social-media platforms. And some food-truck owners will distribute marketing material that drives future sales, such as coupons for redemption after the event.

Chapter Six

Designing the Truck and Menu

When entrepreneurs first visualize their dreams of being food truck owners, those visions often include ideas of how they want their food trucks to look. The food trucks they eventually operate may look dramatically different than what they first visualized, and they may even serve different fare than originally planned. The shift in design is often due to market research, finding their niche in a market, and realizing the regulatory boundaries. Keeping an open mind and not being boxed into one solution will help when creating a business that is efficient and sustainable.

Design the Apparatus

Some factors to consider when designing the apparatus—the structure that will be used to prepare and serve food—are the size limits for the identified locations of service, equipment needed to prepare the menu, and the amount of funding that is both available and worth risking during the startup process. It is common for a food truck entrepreneur to enter the market with future phases in mind. Some will use their learned experiences and realized profits to invest in larger operations or even start brick-and-mortar restaurants. One of the advantages to a food truck is the minimal investment, which means that the investment can be earned back in a relatively short amount of time—and that allows the owner to be versatile when pivoting into larger or simply different business models in the future.

Cost of the apparatus will vary greatly depending on the performance required of it. Food trucks that are all-inclusive of a driving vehicle, storage, prep, and service often range from $25,000 to $200,000. The traditional large carnival trucks will run even higher for an initial investment and require special licenses for hauling. Food carts that are pulled behind a vehicle often range from $10,000 to $50,000 when they are fully equipped and functional. The price of the food cart does not include the price of a vehicle to pull the apparatus. Some owners will choose to use their personal vehicle for hauling while others will either transfer the title of the vehicle to the business or purchase an additional vehicle for pulling the cart. Smaller handcarts can be hauled in manually or on trailers when transporting and can be a lesser investment of $1,000–$15,000 but will require the additional use of a base kitchen or equipment for storing, preparing, and heating the food if a vendor is serving a full menu, not just frozen treats or popcorn.

Looks are not all that matters, though appearance can be a large part of marketing and owning the brand, by connecting branding elements to every facet of the consumer experience. Talking with other food truck owners may save wasted investments and identify lessons they have already learned along the way. Like any industry, some owners may be more willing than others to reveal their findings. Properly designing and equipping an apparatus is paramount to being able to build a successful business. At minimum, the creator will need to make decisions regarding size, fabrication or sourcing, fuel, equipment, appearance and service experience, small wares, and the miscellaneous supplies that will be kept on board.

Meghan Blake-Horst, Street Vending Coordinator for City of Madison, advises that all food truck entrepreneurs should communicate with their local vending coordinators or clerk's offices and with the Department of Health before buying any equipment. The local regulations will dictate what can and cannot be allowed in that area. For instance, some communities have restrictions on how big an apparatus can be, how long it can be parked, where it can be parked, and how obtrusive it can be. Finding and interpreting the regulations can be challenging, so it is important for food truck owners to ask very specific questions often. Because of the growth in popularity of food trucks, many municipalities are updating or creating regulations to protect the industry and community alike.

Size

Restrictions on size may be mandated by the location where service will happen, and size will dictate how much space is available for operating the service-based business. A food cart that is fifty-six square feet can hardly house two people and enough equipment to prepare and serve a menu of five items for a three-hour shift. If a larger capacity is needed, it may be best to consider a food truck that is all-inclusive and has more space for people, equipment, and product. However, the larger an apparatus is, the more costly it can be to purchase and operate, and you may be restricted from serving in certain locations.

When examining empty apparatuses, realize that the space is quickly eaten up by equipment. At minimum, a truck or cart should allow space for immediate storage, cooling, heating, holding, and sanitation. Individuals may able to operate the service shift alone if the equipment layout is efficient and they can reach everything needed without many obstacles to move. The more an item needs to be moved during service, the longer it takes to serve a customer, which means lower volume and revenue will be possible. Additionally, the more often equipment needs to be moved due to learned efficiencies, regulations, or maintenance, the more wear the apparatus will experience. Some trucks are designed to have service panels for built-in equipment, so owners can minimize their downtime when equipment breaks down or lessen their back pain from moving heavy equipment when maintenance needs to be done.

Fabrication and Sourcing

When a fully equipped and functional food truck cannot be found or is not the ideal option for an owner, there are other ways to piece it together. There are fabricators who specialize in building out food trucks, just like there are developers and architects who specialize in designing restaurants. General contractors or skilled workers may also be able to fabricate a food truck into working order if given enough direction and the proper specifications. Some food truck owners prefer to build their own, though, with a lot of sweat equity and a DIY sort of approach. Owners can derive much pride from building out an apparatus on their own. For those building from scratch, many will start with a trailer, bus, or something else on wheels, with various levels of complexity for the buildout.

Insight: Whimsy Dish

Alfonzo Jones III (AJ), is a retired Air Force Chief Master Sergeant who served for over twenty-five years before obtaining his culinary degree and founding Whimsy Dish. Without any additional culinary or for-profit business experience, he started a mobile food business that is still growing three years later. After deciding that the startup of a fully equipped food truck would require $25,000 more financial capital and risk than he was willing to take on, he found a lower-cost entry point that may help him grow the business into the original vision of a food truck.

His eighteen-foot mobile kitchen was purchased for $14,000 before he realized it would need further modification, mostly because it was a gas guzzler. Whimsy Dish has become a hybrid of serving in a traditional food truck style at events and providing hosted catering services. It took AJ two full seasons to refine the model enough to produce a profit. AJ's biggest challenge, predicting the volume of food needed at an event, was partially overcome by installing additional refrigeration units on the apparatus and accessing more storage at his base kitchen.

Whimsy Dish has been able to produce more revenue because of changes to its menu and operation. Rather than making fresh made-to-order hand-cut french fries at events, AJ removed the fryer on board and now puts more emphasis on braised meats, which can be inexpensively prepared at the base kitchen—and that has opened space on the cart and sped up service time per customer. The business has also learned to adapt its menu to capitalize on changing weather, such as serving more soups and fewer sliders on the very chilly fall days, using mostly the same ingredients and equipment as what is usually on board.

Before purchasing or building anything, it is crucial to have communication with the health department and anyone who governs the service area. There is no sense in installing a three-sink setup if the inspector will require a four-sink operation with wing faucets. It happens all the time, though; new food-truck owners will go for inspection and realize that money and resources were wasted because their equipment or operational plans do not meet current or upcoming regulations. Seemingly universal requirements include wipeable, smooth surfaces, NSF-certified equipment, proper water flow and tanks, the ability to cool, heat, and hold at appropriate temperatures, and general safety precautions for operators and public.

Many areas also have standards for noise levels from generators or speakers, fire safety practices and equipment, and even the type of light bulbs that can be used.

Fuel

Experienced food truck owners can be heard talking about fuel as though they carry an advanced degree in such a topic. That is because they often have struggled to find the best option for their operation and have had to quickly become versed in the topic. The best route is dependent on so many factors that there is no right answer that fits everyone, and what works now may change throughout time and as the business serves at new locations or requires different levels of power. It is not common for food-truck businesses to run their entire service locations on solar, but it is common to see them use some solar solutions, such as lights or small solar panels that feed an inverter generator for a single piece of equipment. Because this type of business relies on battling the margins to realize a profit, every efficiency will matter.

Photo Source: Kay-Tee Olds, Madison, WI, 2018.

More common is the use of propane, gas, or electric. Many food trucks operate on propane or a combination of propane with either gas or electric. Those who run on electric should still have a gas or propane backup, since electric can be problematic if too many people are pulling from the grid at a location or if there is a surge that disrupts the flow of energy. Food trucks often strive to be self-sustaining and not reliant on external power sources, so it is not common for an apparatus to be without a generator either for primary or backup energy. Many events and municipalities have restrictions on how much noise a generator can produce, and the price of a generator that can output over two thousand watts, with sixty decibels or less, can quickly grow in cost when compared to its more industrial counterparts. Some businesses will stack inverter generators or split their operation so only essentials would run when relying on generator power. Rather than manually hauling heavy generators or propane tanks around each day, many food trucks have their power sources secured to the exterior of their apparatus, sometimes on the tongue of a trailer where the vehicle and cart can best manage the weight. Others, especially those concerned with theft when the apparatus is parked, will keep their power sources on wheels, to be stored inside the unit when not in use, or have their power sources secured by steel cages. Theft and vandalism are real problems for food truck businesses, which easily become the targets of thieves and jokesters alike. To prevent some of the loss that others experience, some food truck owners are proactive by keeping lights pointed at their equipment, if stored outdoors overnight, and some have monitored security cameras.

Equipment

Purchasing the apparatus, vehicle, and large equipment with a loan or other non-personal funding source will allow the business to minimize the injection of startup cash but may also create pressure on cash flow when repaying the funds. Capital equipment can often be depreciated and provide tax advantages when the business owns it outright rather than renting such equipment. It is not as common for food-truck owners to rent their establishments and large equipment as it would be for a brick-and-mortar restaurant, but it can be done.

Each business has unique equipment needs depending on their anticipated volume, location, and menu. At minimum, the food equipment could include a cooling unit, something to warm food, something to hold the food at temperature, and proper equipment for sanitation. Fryers, ranges, and steam tables are common equipment on trucks. Some equipment options are limited due to lack of ventilation through a hood. Hot boxes and Cambro containers are also common equipment for holding food that was prepared at a base kitchen.

Some investors prefer used equipment, while others may prefer to buy everything new. The advantage of buying new is that some of that equipment may come with warranties and has a better likelihood of operating the way it should for a longer period. However, others may see the advantage of needing less cash to purchase used equipment at startup. When purchasing used equipment, it becomes more important to budget for either higher maintenance expenses or future replacement of equipment after the business is generating revenue. Since food trucks often generate only enough money to pay off expenses and employ one or two full-time employees (FTEs) during the initial years, the restricted cash-flow budget should be considered when deciding how much to invest upfront and what the repayment terms will be for any monies borrowed. More money invested means either an added drain on cash flow when repaying loans or at least a longer period to endure before a return on the investment can be realized.

Caution should be practiced when purchasing equipment. Consider the layout of all equipment. Securing equipment to the apparatus will improve safety and protect the equipment during transit. Experienced food truck owners such as Thony Clarke, fifteen-year owner of the Café Costa Rica food cart, will advise that—like any ingredient on the cart—every piece of equipment should be used for at least three purposes, or it is not worth the space it takes up. That could affect how the menu is formulated and may help when deciding between equipment options. The challenge of piecing together equipment from different sources is a large part of why some start-ups will decide to purchase a ready-for-service apparatus. Refer to Chapter Three for tips on common regulations and required equipment.

Like vehicles and food carts, equipment can be procured as used or new. Used equipment can be found online, through shared kitchens, and through used dealers. New equipment can be purchased through equipment brokers, who often demonstrate their equipment at food shows and may be willing to arrange personal demonstrations. Water tanks can be purchased through RV dealers or sometimes through home-improvement stores. Propane tanks are easily found used online or new at propane retailers. Generators can be found used or new through retailers that specialize in power equipment.

Insight: Totally Awesome Vegan Food Truck

Photo Courtesy of: Totally Awesome Vegan Food Truck, Portland Maine.

Tony Diphillipo, owner of the Totally Awesome Vegan Food Truck in Portland, Maine, stated that he had underestimated the need for steam tables and hot holding, so he can keep more stuff that can hold hot, like toppings and sauces, which really helps with the speed. Diphillipo said that it takes time to cook stuff over the grill, but stuff in the hot holding is just ready to serve.

Having started the Totally Awesome Vegan Food Truck in the summer of 2018, Tony found the learning curve to be steep. However, he encourages aspiring entrepreneurs to take the dive and not look back if this is something they really want to do.

Appearance and Service

Ever wonder why some food trucks attract more customers than others? The appearance may have everything to do with it, sometimes more than the menu. A truck with a small one-foot window may not be as inviting as one that has a four-foot window. A food truck that looks like it is falling apart and rusting or molding at the seams may trigger a thought from passersby that it is not a clean or safe option for dining. Another error that is common of food trucks is having an illegible menu, unclear pricing, or confusing menu items that do not make sense at a glance without further explanation.

The branding and design of a food truck can support its brand and continue the process of creating a unique customer experience, or it can do the opposite and work against the business's perceived value. Many businesses will invest in graphic design and professional wrap or painting. Some may only brand the front of their vehicle, the side where customers receive service. However, many take advantage of their entire footprint since the apparatus can be a moving billboard during transport. Lights are more than a functional piece of equipment. They can be used to create a warm and inviting presence during dusk or dark hours. Proper lighting of the apparatus, people in the truck, and its menu can give a business the advantage over neighboring food vendors.

While some areas will restrict a food truck to its original

footprint, others allow for expanded service space. That means that a truck could have shutters that fold down and double as service or dining counters. Trailers with dropdown back doors can be supported to create a flat platform for production or display. Other businesses may haul foldable tables and chairs to create small café dining areas near their truck. Canopies or umbrellas are common extensions for food trucks to protect servers or diners from the weather elements.

Small Wares and Miscellaneous

Just when it seems that equipment expenses are adding up, it is time to account for the numerous pieces of small ware that a food truck requires. Purchasing duplicates of everything and etching a name or symbol into each piece will save money and headaches during the busiest of days so that utensils do not get lost or grow legs and walk away. Portion-control scoops will help control the margins during quick service of customers, and a sanitation method on board will prevent cross-contamination— or at the very least prevent the unnecessary scrubbing of caked-on product when returning to the base kitchen. When looking for used hotel pans, serving scoops, or pots, keep an eye out for going-out-of-business sales. They happen all the time, unfortunately, since restaurant startups are a risky business and often need to liquidate their inventory to pay off debts if the business flips upside down.

Even with the most detailed plan for equipment, small ware, and basic supplies to start up the operation on a food truck, there will be more needed. Budgeting 150 percent of the planned expense for miscellaneous materials needed may be appropriate. Plan for the simple things, like garbage cans, fire extinguishers, a lifetime supply of zip ties, brooms, mops, rags, fans, can openers, knives, first-aid supplies, tension tie downs, and tire blocks. Supplies, unlike equipment, will be continuously consumed and replaced but will incur a larger expense at startup, because there is no starting inventory when beginning a business. Plan for increased supply expenses in the first quarter to order cases of gloves, disposables, soaps and detergents, uniforms, paper products, tinfoil and Saran Wrap, seasonings, squeeze bottles, storage containers, and tape.

Selecting a Commissary Kitchen

Some areas of the country refer to the commissary kitchen as a *base kitchen* or *commissary*; both meaning the same thing. Determining where base-kitchen operations will occur may have a direct impact on the type of equipment needed on board, the inventory-ordering process, and the preparation schedule. The decision will most certainly affect the bottom line. Some food trucks are operated by brick-and-mortar restaurants, and they often have less direct costs related to a base kitchen than a stand-alone truck that needs to buy or rent the space from a third party. Some food trucks share commercial kitchens rather than buying or leasing their own base-kitchen space. Sharing space can eliminate the need to purchase kitchen equipment such as ranges, hood systems, dishwashers, and the other equipment common to a commercial kitchen. Independent kitchens require additional insurance, buildout costs, and maintenance that would otherwise be assumed by the entity managing the shared kitchen. Makers may share kitchen space with a church, community center, another restaurant, or multiple food-production businesses. Wherever the base-kitchen operations occur, the space needs to be licensed by the Department of Health or similar governing body.

Insight: FEED Kitchens, a Shared Commercial-Kitchen Incubator

Chris Brockel is the Operations Coordinator of FEED Kitchens, which is a shared-use commercial-kitchen business incubator. Brockel provides day-to-day support to food entrepreneurs working at FEED, including intake and orientation to the facility, licensing support, troubleshooting issues, ingredient sourcing, scheduling, referrals to business-support services, and a shoulder to lean on. Businesses working out of FEED Kitchens include food carts, caterers, bakers, value-added processors, farm-to-table efforts, and a variety of community-based projects. During an interview for this book, Brockel shared insights into the food truck space that helped define the experience people have with shared kitchens, while highlighting some of the challenges and opportunities that seem prevalent across several micro-businesses that want to start or grow a food truck business.

Money, and the lack of access to or management of it, is at the root of many challenges he helps food truck owners through. There may be a perception that food trucks are cheap and easy to start, but many never make it to opening day, or much past that point. They simply run out of money during the startup process or during their first setbacks. Of the fifty to seventy aspiring entrepreneurs that attend information workshops at FEED annually, only about 20–25 percent open their business. At any given time, the shared kitchen will have ten to twenty food trucks operating out of it, in addition to the other makers using the space. For a fee of approximately $6,500 per year, a food truck business uses the base kitchen anywhere from two to six hours per day.

During off-seasons, food trucks may still use the kitchen to create additional streams of revenue by offering catering or value-added products such as chips, salsas, and jams. Brockel recognizes that the industry has two significant threats that could disrupt the food truck scene but not directly affect those additional product offerings: the threat of saturation and the threat of bad publicity caused by an operator, which could affect the public's perception of food trucks collectively. Consider how consumers react to a recall or safety announcement about a product and how that entire industry is affected. For instance, if ground turkey were recalled from one manufacturer, people may subconsciously start to worry about all forms of turkey products, which could be especially detrimental if it happened near a peak selling period; the same could happen if a food truck were to create a health concern.

Menu Design

Alas, the section about menu creation! Many food truck startups look forward to sharing their culinary skills and creating that memorable dish that lines of customers cannot resist. Keep in mind, the menu should support the brand and provide for efficient ordering, prep, and service. If the theme of a truck is Indian cuisine, then rice could be an efficient product to incorporate into several menu items. A pizza truck may rely on a limited number of crust types but vary the toppings and sauces. Similarly, a panini truck can keep its inventory cost and waste at bay by creating several menu items from the same base but changing up the toppings and sauces. Remember, there is only so much space on a food truck or food cart, so everything on that apparatus must be worth the real estate it uses.

Calculating the real costs of the menu will help keep the expense ratios intact. Restaurants and mobile food vendors can find a profit if labor and supplies are kept below 60 percent. That usually means that chefs will spend 25–30 percent of revenue on cost of goods sold or on the food and packaging supplies. Spending significantly less than that may sacrifice quality beyond the point of value control, but businesses spending more than that tend to operate in the red. Because many food trucks will adjust retail pricing and serving sizes for different venues, the ratio may vary, but the average is likely to come in near the 25–30 percent mark. Figuring out the real cost of a menu item involves creating or finding a recipe, sourcing the supplies needed to create and package the menu item, and then calculating exactly how much that serving cost to make. There are some programs available online and through food distributors that will help to calculate the real cost of a menu item by using software. Either the software or the person should calculate what percent of a product, such as a bag of rice, was used in making that serving. Then multiply the cost of that bag by the percent used for a serving.

Waste, sanity, and time should be accounted for when considering the real cost of a product. The shorter shelf life a product or its ingredients has, the more waste or more frequent ordering will occur. If a batch of ingredients creates ten servings but only nine are usually sold on average, then the cost of that one wasted item should be accounted for when costing the production of a menu item. Someone may ask why the business wouldn't simply make nine instead of ten. While that is an option in some cases, the manager may choose to make all ten because nine is an average, and sometimes that tenth item is sold, or because the ingredients are perishable, and so they would be wasted whether in raw or finished form.

Customer feedback is an important part of the process when creating a menu. If the business is already in operation, a new product can be tested in the market by adding it as a daily special. Startups may need to take their product to a group of people, an informal focus group, to receive feedback on appearance, taste, price, and general appeal. Getting people to sample a menu item is much easier than finding volunteer focus groups for other products, so this is a viable form of inexpensive research before adding a product to the menu.

Many restauranteurs with small menus will have a couple staple or iconic items that are always present, but then supplement with items that are seasonal or simply exciting because they are different. This allows for efficiency in ordering and preparation but also keeps the menu fresh for staff and customers alike. Food trucks are often independently owned businesses that do not need to follow franchise rules or menus dictated by a far-removed parent company. That means that when a certain type of produce is in season, or a supplier runs a significant discount on a product, the chef can create a custom dish to feature such an item and keep it on the menu for a limited time. It is important to remember that every ingredient on the food truck should have more than one purpose to justify commanding the real estate—mentally, physically, and financially—that it consumes.

People eat with their eyes and nose. Even though roasted chicken and garlic mashed potatoes are both delicious, they may not be the best pair for appearance on a plate. The eyes are drawn to meals that help them eat the rainbow. Contrasting colors can improve the customer experience and increase the chance that they will share a photo of that dish on social media and that the photo will be a positive representation of the business. Also consider how packaging affects the perceived value of a dish. Paper boats, two- or three-compartment plates or clams (to-go containers with hinged lids), and disposable plates are commonly used to serve street-fare meals. The material, color, and functionality will matter, so consider those elements when comparing options and prices. Applying various flavor profiles can keep the menu exciting for diners without creating a lot of additional cost and inventory needs for the purveyor. Keep in mind that preference and tolerance of spice may vary by region or demographics. Heat can be added by customers using sauces but cannot easily diluted or removed once a product is prepared. Finding that fine balance of being flavorful is an art. For owners who lack a culinary background, there is training available through various outlets, or they may decide to hire a consultant or chef to design the recipes and menu.

Food allergies effect 15 million Americans and that number continues to climb. A 2013 Centers for Disease Control and Prevention study measured the growth of allergies in children from 1997 to 2011 and found that food allergies grew 50% in children during that time span.[13] Gluten-free and "free-from" foods are in-demand. Statista reports $0.9 billion in such foods were purchased in 2006 and the expectation is that the same food categories will command $23.9 billion in 2020, in the U.S.[14] With increased consumer focus on nutritional values and limited diets, food-service companies are being challenged further with menu creation. Vegetarians, vegans,

---

13 McKeever, Amy. "How Restaurant Pros Are Handling the Surge of Food Allergies." Eater. June 19, 2014. Accessed March 22, 2019. https://www.eater.com/2014/6/19/6207199/how-restaurant-pros-are-handling-the-surge-of-food-allergies.

14 Whitehead, S.A. "Why Gluten-free Isn't a Dying Trend." Www.fastcasual.com. January 13, 2017. Accessed March 22, 2019. https://www.fastcasual.com/articles/why-gluten-free-isnt-a-dying-trend/.

and pescatarians are only a few of the dietary groups that will be present when serving mass crowds. It is becoming more common to hear questions about gluten, paleo, nuts, and lactose from customers. There is a sense of frustration from the culinary community because much pride and time goes into the creation of a menu and then the sourcing and preparation of it. However, some food trucks are embracing the special diet needs and capitalizing on them financially by building their brand or menu to satisfy the desires of customers with special diet request.

Menu creation does not end once the recipes, research, sourcing, and production are complete. The marketing elements of the menu continue. Creating a menu that is legible can require the work of a graphic artist or some of the numerous software or mobile apps that allow any common person to create semi-professional-looking material. A menu with more than four to six food items can be confusing or give too many options when a passerby sees it. A lengthy menu can also be cumbersome for operators because they must source, prepare, and hold all those ingredients and still try to spend less than two minutes with a customer at the window. That time at the window is also taken up by indecisiveness and transacting money. Some mobile food vendors will opt for a dry-erase board or chalkboard so they can change their menu regularly. That media may work if the vendor has good handwriting skills. Others may choose to have slots build into a board, so they can print a menu item and price to slide into the slot for that day. And others may have multiple menu items and prices printed professionally so they can display them on any given day. Most important is to remember that the menu is a valuable component of direct marketing; it should be clean, professional, legible from a distance, and a continuation of the brand.

Sourcing the Menu

Convenience, quality, and cost are some of the primary factors to consider when deciding how to source supplies for creating a menu. Traditionally, restauranteurs work with food distributors that deliver products to their door on a regular basis. Some food trucks go that route, which can be convenient but come at a cost. Others work directly with local producers when possible, which can add a fresh flare to their menu but also come at the cost of additional needed to work with multiple suppliers. And some run to retail locations and buy on demand.

When food truck owners work with food distributors, products are often procured by the case or other bulk-volume metrics. Each distributor will operate on different terms, and so the owner should be prepared for cash in advance, net seven, or net thirty-day terms. Setting up an account usually involves a credit application, which can require financial information about the business and sometimes about the owner(s). Once the distributor's finance department evaluates the credit application, terms are presented. Delivery schedules and minimums may vary from one distributor to another. The order minimums are a deterrent for some food trucks because they simply do not churn enough volume to command a convenient or free delivery of goods. The process of placing an order may include calling in to a representative that was assigned to the account, ordering through an online system or mobile application, or placing the next order with the delivery representative when they are delivering the previous order. Some distributors also host food shows where buyers can sample products from various brokers or manufacturers, either for future orders or for ordering on-site. The obvious advantage of working with a distributor is the convenience. However, do not be surprised when prices tend to change without notice or not be published, since the pricing may vary between time periods or even between two like customers. Most distributors will prefer to be exclusive for a customer, but most buyers will prefer having accounts with two or three distributors, either to keep competitive pricing or to ensure a product is always available, in case it is delayed or not available from one.

Shopping retail stores for a product can help keep the total cost down during initial orders, because a business could buy one #10 can of a product rather than six in a case. However, it also means running around to stores during an already busy day. Discount stores and warehouses may recognize tax-exempt statuses while others are not set up to do so and will charge the sales tax on a product intended for resale. One of the health concerns with this process is that most buyers who run around to buy on demand from retail stores are not equipped to safely transport temperature-sensitive goods. While some food-truck owners may purchase their packaging and shelf-stable products in person, others will order online, just like a consumer would shop the online retailers. And others may shop at local markets or produce auctions such as the one pictured below.

Photo Source: Kay-Tee Olds, Tri-County Produce Auction, Dalton WI, Summer, 2018.

Mobile foodservice businesses commonly work with other locally owned businesses or organizations to source local products or unique value-added items. Another way they work together is by cross-promoting each other's products. A food truck may carry another company's hot sauce and promote that fact while the sauce maker promotes how to find their sauce at that truck's locations. Produce auctions offer a convenient and exciting method for sourcing perishable products from multiple local vendors.

Ordering or buying in real-time can save on waste and keep orders smaller in cost, at the expense of time and the risk of not being able to source a product when it's needed. If you are ordering in bulk, it becomes more important to practice First In, First Out (FIFO), so products are constantly being rotated. Similarly, it is important to label and date everything, which is also required by health-department inspectors.

Chapter Seven

Financial Projections and Management

Financial management is the backbone of any business. During the business-planning process, it is important to prepare financial projections that are realistic. This includes estimating expenses and income, as well as planning how the cash and debt will be managed. Financial documents may be viewed later by lenders or investors. Even if the founder of a business is planning to personally finance the startup, financial documents will be needed to calculate cash needed and project cash flow of operations.

Financial Documents

Entrepreneurs who lack experience with financial management, business management, or business ownership may be overwhelmed by where to start and how to prepare proper financial documents. The process can be made easier by starting with templates and plugging in numbers. Keep in mind that the process will require a trial-and-error mindset as the numbers are manipulated to be inclusive of all functions, to paint a full financial picture of the business. It is rare to create a final set of financial projections in an initial attempt. It usually takes several edits and the incorporation of feedback from advisors or updates discovered while working through the other components of planning a business. In the end, financial projections and plans for financial management should create a framework for funding the business and operating it within a budget, and they should provide a mechanism for evaluating when financial results create a red flag, to alert a manager to potential dangers.

Start-Up Financial Documents:

- Startup costs worksheet
- Cash-flow projection
- Projected profit and loss statement
- Projected balance sheet
- Sources and uses of funds statement

Statement Order

Start the process by creating a startup costs worksheet. The challenge will lie within the lack of data, since many of the numbers on a startup costs worksheet will be estimates—though some of the mystery can be removed by contacting vendors and requesting quotes. From there, create a cash-flow projection, which will require data from the estimated costs and startup cash. Estimate the amount of cash you will need, since that number can be adjusted throughout the creation of financial projections. A projected profit and loss statement can only be created after the cash-flow worksheet, since it will rely on data derived from that worksheet. Then a projected balance sheet can be created, which will be complemented by the creation of a sources and uses of funds statement. Lenders will especially want to see the cash-flow worksheet, projected profit and loss statement, and beginning balance sheet. Some templates, including the one provided as an addendum to this book, will allow for several of the statements to auto populate as data is calculated in a corresponding cell on another Excel worksheet. Simple conveniences like that auto populated data will eliminate some human error and streamline the process of working with numbers that will continue to be adjusted while affecting other statements.

Budget and Cash Flow

Lenders will want to see a budget, often referred to as a cash-flow statement or projection. This document will show how much money you need to make to cover the expenses (working capital) and what the expenses are each month. Typically, a cash-flow statement will be categorized by month and then by year, for up to three years.

Some things to think about before you begin:

- What do you need before opening the doors of your business?
- What will your fixed and variable experiences be on a continuing basis?
- What can you contribute to keep costs low?
- What can you get donated by people you know?

- What can you live without?

The less cash you spend at startup, without creating ineffi-ciencies, the sooner you can start making a profit.

Step 1—Plan for Opening Day

This does not mean to plan for a large celebration. Begin by determining what you will need on the opening day of your business to produce your product, welcome custom-ers, and manage transactions.

An opening-day budget may include four general categories:

- **Facilities:** This includes your base kitchen, food truck, buildout or fabrication, and major signage. Costs may include purchases and deposits.
- **Fixed assets**: These assets are often referred to as capital expenditures. They could include major equipment such as cooking or warming equipment, generators, and coolers.
- **Supplies:** Consider all the consumable supplies needed for operating the business, preparing food products, and serving them. Examples would be disposable containers, paper goods, seasonings, all ingredients for the menu, soaps, and disposable gloves.
- **Other necessary costs:** This could include licenses, permits, insurance premiums, legal fees, or POS subscriptions.

Be sure to include items that you are personally

providing to the business, such as office furniture, computer and printer, cookware, and other equipment. Such items will appear as a credit under collateral.

Step 2—Estimate Monthly Expenses

Both fixed and variable expenses should be accounted for. These expenses are not unique to opening day but rather will be ongoing expenses every month. Fixed expenses are not dependent on the volume of sales or how many customers you serve. Variable expenses are dependent on volume and will increase as the business grows and serves more people. Some people find it helpful to asses a percent of revenue to variable costs. That method can help create close to accurate estimates of variable expenses so the estimated costs of a line item can be automatically adjusted for if the revenue estimates change throughout the process of creating financial projections.

Fixed Expenses Examples:

- Rent for the base kitchen (if it's a flat fee; if it is by the hour, then it is a variable expense)
- Utilities
- Phones (business phones and cell phones)
- Credit-card processing—monthly subscription fees (transaction fees are variable)
- Website service or subscription fees
- Equipment-lease payments
- Office supplies
- Dues/subscriptions

- Advertising, publicity, and promotion commitments, like social media or online ads
- Business insurance
- Professional fees (legal and accounting)
- Employee pay/benefits (if salaried or relied on regardless of sales volume)
- Business-loan payments
- Licensing and permit fees

Variable Expenses Examples:

- Hourly wage and payroll expenses (for employees who are added to the schedule, beyond minimum coverage of duties)
- Consumable inventory
- Food supplies
- Packaging supplies
- Fuel
- Credit-card transaction fees (different than the monthly subscription or software cost)
- Sales tax (record in the month it will be paid)

Step 3—Estimate Monthly Revenue

This could be the most challenging estimate because it is impossible to know exactly what the sales will be. Speaking with other food truck operators may be helpful to determine what an average day of sales could be. Remember to adjust for key events that could bring in dramatic increases of revenue or bad-weather days that could stunt sales. A tip would be to underestimate sales, so the bottom line is not cushioned by unrealistic or unachievable total revenue numbers. It would not be realistic to estimate the same revenue in each month. Peak-season months' revenue will be higher than that of slow months and the initial months of any business are likely to produce less revenue than future months. Monthly revenue may also be dependent on weather, foot traffic, or other location-related factors. The first month of sales will rarely be as high as that of future months, even if it is a peak season, since it takes time to attract customers and operate efficiently enough to run at full capacity.

To be realistic when budgeting, assume that not all sales will be collected. Depending on the way customers pay, you might have a greater or smaller losses related to the collection process. Credit cards can bounce, especially if you are transacting offline, and then become a charge-back. It is rare for food trucks to accept personal checks, but if they do, there will also be a percent of checks that will come back returned due to insufficient funds or other reasons. A food truck business that provides group sales, catering, or wholesale may also experience collection challenges if money is not received in advance of providing the product or service.

Add the variable and fixed expenses for each month to find the sum of the monthly expenses. It will be helpful for business leaders and their lenders to calculate a break-even point. A break-even analysis shows a lender when the business will start to create a profit. Business owners need to know what their break-even point is to properly manage their money. Such knowledge is especially helpful considering new products or pivotal decisions in the business. A break-even analysis can determine how much funding may be needed to cover a financial gap during growth periods as well.[15] A simple equation can be used when trying to figure out how many units will need to be sold for the revenue to surpass the expenses.

Fixed Costs / (Price–Variable Costs) = Break-Even Units

If a food cart sells 75 meals per day, at $10 per meal, it does mean that the owner will profit $750 that day. For instance, if they have $5,000 of fixed expenses each month and estimate that each $10 meal has variable costs of $3, then they would need to sell 715 meals before realizing any profit. An example of the break-even equation, when applied to a food truck, could be viewed as the following, ignoring the need for currency symbols:

*5,000 / (10–3) = 715 meals would
need to be sold to break even*

When there are multiple variables to account for, such as multiple products or price points to consider, a spreadsheet that can be translated to a graph may be more helpful. The spreadsheet will plot break-even points for each level of sales and product price and can then be viewed as a graph, demonstrating the break-even for each of the prices and sales volumes.

---

15 Murray, Jean. "5 Easy Steps to Creating a Break-even Analysis." The Balance Small Business. Accessed March 22, 2019. https://www.thebalancesmb.com/how-to-do-a-break-even-analysis-398032.

Step 4—Create a Cash-Flow Statement

Use the data from steps one through three to create a cash-flow statement in brief. Here is an example of how that could be formatted for a given month:

- Monthly sales: $10,000
- Collected: $9,900
- Total fixed costs: $5,000
- Total variable costs: $3,800
- Total cash balance: $1,100

The $1,100 represents your total cash balance for the month. That does not mean that your realized or taxable profit will be $1,100 per month or $13,200 for the year.

Manipulating these numbers in the cash-flow summary will allow for alternate scenarios to be calculated. It may also help the organization to realize the cash needed, either from the owner or other funding sources, to sustain the business operations, also referred to as working capital, until the business starts to create a healthy flow of cash on its own.

The cash-flow summary can be included in an executive-brief section of a business plan to provide a glance at the cash needs for a business. A more detailed worksheet should be used to create the actual cash-flow statement and that will differentiate where the revenue is coming from and where the expenses are going to, using the data from Steps Two and Three of this step-by-step process.

Year 1 Cash Flow

Year 1	Pre-Start	1	2
Receipts			
Revenue Line 1	0		
Revenue Line 2	0		
Revenue Line 3	0		
Revenue Line 4	0		
Owner's Investment	0		
Total Receipts	**0**	**0**	**0**
Payments			
Food Supplies (COGS)	0		
Nonfood Supplies (COGS)	0		
Credit Card & Merchant Fees	0		
Rent and Storage	0		

Total Payments		0	0
Cashflow Surplus/Deficit (-)		0	0
Opening Cash Balance		0	0
Closing Cash Balance		0	0

Image Source: Cash Flow Statement originated from WWBIC and was then edited to fit food truck needs, by Mobile Contessa Media, 2018.

Access full template at mobilecontessa.com/business-essentials/ cash-flow-projection-profitloss-statement-worksheet

A three-year cash-flow worksheet will keep a running count of available cash as each month's activity is added to the starting balance. Businesses may keep their cash-flow projections updated so they can anticipate when significant surpluses or deficits will occur. Seasonal businesses, such as many food trucks, may end peak seasons with a significant surplus but realize when looking ahead on their cash-flow projections that they may need to dip into reserves or secure funding to survive through down seasons. Remember that fixed costs, including insurance premiums, loan repayments, and sometimes rent payments, will continue whether the business is producing revenue or not in each month. When surpluses are realized for several consecutive months, a business may consider building a separate reserve fund, paying out draws to owners, providing bonuses to employees, or changing the purchasing process to pay larger advance payments to vendors and receive discounts for doing so.

Beginning Balance Sheet

Startup businesses do not have a financial history, and that makes a beginning balance sheet even more important to a lender. The balance sheet will be used to show the financial position, including what already occurred during planning stages and what will happen before opening day. This financial document will show the assets, liabilities, and equities, more simply explained as what the business owns and what it owes. It will be calculated for a specific moment in time.

There are two columns on the balance sheet, with assets on the left and liabilities and owner's equity on the right. The reason it is called a balance sheet is because the **total assets must equal total liabilities + total owner equity** (or *retained earnings* for a corporation); that is the premise of accounting and its most principle formula. The calculations of a beginning spreadsheet should reflect the current state of financial strength. A startup may also prepare a projected balance sheet to show where the business will be at opening day.

When you present a beginning balance sheet to a lender or investor, it may be helpful to provide two versions: one that reflects a cash injection from the loan and the other without. Here is an example of a simplified balance sheet for a food truck, showing the difference with or without a loan:

Before the Loan

The owner has already put $13,000 into the business for cash, prepaid insurance, and equipment.

Assets		Liabilities and owner's equity	
Cash	$ 3,500	Current liabilities	$1,000
Inventory	$ 0	Loans and long-term liabilities	$0
Prepaid insurance	$ 2,500		
Cart (not food truck	$ 8,000	Owner's equity	$13,000
Total assets	$ 14,000	Total liabilities and owner's Equity	$14,000

After the Loan

The second balance shows a $50,000 loan, which is being used to buy a ready-to-operate food truck and starting inventory.

Assets		Liabilities and owner's equity	
Cash	$1,500	Current liabilities	$1,000
Inventory	$10,000	Loans and long-term liabilities	$50,000
Prepaid insurance	$2,500		
Food truck	$40,000	Owner's equity	$13,000
Kitchen equipment	$10,000		
Total assets	$64,000	Total liabilities and owner's Equity	$64,000

Many small-business owners will require the help of a certified public accountant (CPA) to create a balance sheet. Even if a manager relies on a bookkeeper or accountant to handle daily bookkeeping functions, it is important that the owner or senior manager is reviewing financial reports at least quarterly if not monthly, to keep a firm grasp on financial performance. Being able to read financial reports and evaluate them for accuracy or significant variances is a crucial skill for any business owner. For that reason, first-time entrepreneurs can benefit from formal training and business-related financial management education.

Profit and Loss Statement

Also referred to as an income statement, this document will show the results of profits and losses over a specific time. Such a document can help track the progress and keep a close eye on the ever-changing health of a business. Unlike a cash-flow statement, it looks at bottom line rather than top line. Every business should prepare and review its profit and loss statement periodically—at least every quarter. Reviewing the profit and loss statement helps the managers to make decisions and the CPA to prepare the business tax return. For most independently owned businesses that are not setup as corporations, the P&L statement will be directly linked to the amount of income tax the owner(s) will be responsible for.

After completing the monthly budget and knowing the starting cash, a P&L or income statement can be projected for the first year. New businesses will create this statement pro forma, which means that it is projected into the future. The pro forma P&L statement will be required of most lenders.

P&L Statement

Image Source: Cash Flow Statement originated from WWBIC and was then edited to fit food truck needs, by Mobile Contessa Media, 2018.

Access full template at mobilecontessa.com/business-essentials/ cash-flow-projection-profitloss-statement-worksheet

To create the pro forma P&L statement, you will need:

1. A listing of all expense transactions that ran through any of your accounts, including checking, credit card, and barter. Do not forget to account for any purchases made with petty cash.

2. The income side will need transaction information from all revenue received, including any cash received.

3. All redemptions of discounts will also be import-
    ant, so track loyalty rewards, coupons, and other
    discounts.

Start by listing your business income for each quarter of
the year, which will be broken down into finer categorie-
ries, such as lunch service versus special-event income—
or any categories that may help when determining what
about the business is flailing or exceling. Then itemize
the expenses per quarter and show them as a percent. For
instance, you may determine that food supplies are 25
percent of business income or revenue. Knowing the percent will help when predicting future performance. Then
show the difference between sales and expenses as earnings, also referred to as EBITDA (earnings before interest,
taxes, depreciation, amortization).

Most small-business owners will rely on contracted
bookkeepers or volunteer advisors to help them with the
next steps: to show total interest on your business debt for
the year and to subtract that from EBITDA. Then list taxes
on net income (usually estimated) and subtract. Next, show
total depreciation and amortization for the year and subtract. The result you have now is net earnings. The final net
earnings would be the actual profit or loss of the business.

Others may find the final net loss or profit of the
business by calculating it manually or using accounting software. Those who calculate it manually often use
spreadsheets in Excel and have received formal training.
Most software programs have prompts to work through,
to input the appropriate data for the program to prepare
the report and findings.

Preparing the pro forma P&L statement can be challenging since most of the numbers will merely be estimates. It is easiest to prepare the document after creating a realistic cash-flow pro forma, remembering to overestimate expenses and underestimate revenues. The P&L statement provided as an addendum syncs directly with the provided cash-flow statement, so when one is manipulated, the other automatically experiences changes as well.

Sources and Uses of Funds Statement

Unlike a large corporation that will include a lengthy source and uses of funds statement in its annual report, an independently owned food truck can usually opt for a simple list of sources and uses. The list will basically show what collateral you are bringing into the business and what you need to spend on. In other words, how much you need and what you need it for. Creating a sources and uses statement is helpful for meetings with lenders but also a good way to get creative on finding ways to finance your business startup.

Sample Sources and Uses of Funds Statement

Uses of Funds:
Facilities costs: $6,000
Equipment and vehicles: $55,000
Supplies and advertising: $2,000
Other start-up costs: $1,500
Total startup costs: $64,500
Working capital required: $30,000

Total uses of funds: $94,500

Sources of Funds:
Owner collateral:
IRA: $50,000
Owner savings: $10,000
Line of credit: $10,000
Total collateral: $70,000

Total to Be Financed: $24,500

Total Sources of Cash: $94,500

The sources and uses statement does not have to be complicated. Remember to include the costs of obtaining funding sources in your uses of funds section. Be as accurate and complete as you can be and leave nothing unaccounted for. Food truck owners may work through the unpredictable days with ease, but lenders notoriously frown at surprises.

Measure What Matters

There is a difference between leading and lagging indicators, and while it is easy to get distracted by the former, it is the latter that will tell the story of how the business is performing. Leading indicators are the factors that lead to future results and are usually a means to another end. For instance, the number of social-media followers a business has or the number of events that a food truck applies for are leading indicators and have a direct influence on future results, but they do not tell the story of current results. Realized revenue, the number of customers who purchased in the last month, and the net profit of a business are examples of lagging indicators. They were affected by their corresponding leading indicators but are more telling of the results of a business. Accounting tends to look backward and focuses on lagging indicators. It is easy to focus on the tasks that lead to results, but regardless of how well those are performing, a business's bottom line and the end results of a period are the final lagging results.

Financial Planning

Planning financials goes beyond the startup phase. It is important to plan for long-term financial needs. Food trucks find their profits in the margins, and the profitability of a business will affect both the business and the owner's financial health. Managing the income will help you understand how much money will be needed for tax payments, monthly expenses, and reserve accounts. Cash-flow projections look at the timeliness of income and expenses, since an annual profit does not necessarily mean that the business will have enough cash on hand when it is needed throughout the year. Having adequate capital in the business can improve the ability to act on opportunities. It is important to have a solid understanding of the business's financial standing to properly manage its cash and assets while also avoiding burden of liabilities. Financial planning should be a consideration when planning for utilization of accounting software, reporting to shareholders, understanding the reports, POS management, and managing theft/security risks.

Using Accounting Software

Many small businesses, including food trucks, use accounting software to manage their money transactions and keep track of financial performance. Programs like QuickBooks and Wave can help a business owner manage daily financial activity and then automate the process of producing the reports needed to evaluate performance and report to agencies such as the IRS or state departments of revenue. It can be easy to get lost in the nitty-gritty of managing financial activity and to forget to view it strategically. Reviewing regular performance reports, such as a P&L or aging report, can help a business owner keep a handle on what the data means. QuickBooks is the most popular accounting software for small businesses to use, and it comes with either a purchase or subscription fee. Operating the program also requires self-education or formal training, as the program is so robust that it can be confusing to set up and operate if the individual does not have experience with the program. Wave is one of the competing programs, and while it is not as robust as QuickBooks, it can be easier and free to use for the needs of a simple business such as a food truck. There are other software options available for purchase or subscription, so the entrepreneur should consider which program will best fit the needs and skills of the person who will be operating it.

Financial Reports

Shareholders should be provided financial reports on a regular basis, often quarterly and always at least annually. The reports should provide enough accurate information for the recipient to understand the financial status of the business and its financial strengths and weaknesses. The reports should also present new or corrected information from previous reports. The basic forms in a financial report include a P&L statement, a balance sheet, and a summary of strategies. If the owner is not the person managing the bookkeeping of the business, the bookkeeper should produce reports for the owner on a regular basis. For checks and balances, there should also be a policy in place to protect or catch errors and mishandlings.

Point of Sale

VentureCapital.org mentor Michael Flint writes that an estimated 82 percent of businesses fail because of "poor cash flow management skills/poor understanding of cash flow."[16] The speed and cost to accept payments from customers should be considered by food truck owners so they can capture as much revenue as possible, at the fastest and least expensive rate available. Some mobile food vendors still operate on a cash-only basis, but most are now accepting credit cards and some even accept mobile payment. The businesses that only accept cash may be trying

---

16 Flint, Michael. "Cash Flow: The Reason 82% of Small Businesses Fail." Preferred CFO. September 13, 2018. Accessed March 21, 2019. https:// www.preferredcfo.com/cash-flow-reason-small-businesses-fail/.

to hide some of their revenue from financial reports, to reduce their taxable income. However, they also lose track of their actual financial performance and increase the invitation of theft from employees by doing so. Operating an adequate system for processing transactions and tracking inventory and labor can reduce waste and theft.

There are robust point-of-sale systems that can track inventory, employee time clocks, and the profitability of specific menu items. Such programs usually come with initial setup or hardware fees, coupled with monthly subscription and payment-processing fees. For a food truck that is running at full capacity and transacting more than $5,000 per month from credit cards, the robust programs may be the most efficient, since the related merchant service provider often provides lower processing fees than plug-and-play systems and can help the owner manage other areas of the business that require waste or theft reduction. Common programs may include ShopKeep, Revel, and TouchBistro, which all require an iPad or similar device and a proprietary card reader, and all operate through a touchpad that allows the business to navigate various management and transaction systems within the dashboard. However, a break-even analysis should be performed to determine if the benefits of such a program offset the associated costs. Other options, which often come with fewer costs for startup but higher processing or subscription fees, are available. Some food trucks that transact a minimal amount through credit cards may opt to use a plug-and-play option such as Square, PayPal, or Clover, which do not require setup or hardware fees for the initial unit. Since food trucks often operate at various locations throughout the year, or even in a given week, connectivity should be considered. Hard connection to fiber, phone lines, or any internet service is likely not available. Wi-Fi or mobile data may be available in some areas, but some service areas may not have direct access to any connectivity. When operating a POS remotely, without connectivity, the business will run a risk of chargebacks if a card is later discovered to be rejected, once the hardware is back online. To combat that, some food-truck owners will post a policy of not allowing credit-card payments over a specific amount, or they may have a backup method for processing the payment, such as running a card reader on a phone that uses a different carrier so their chance of having connectivity on one or the other is increased.

Some factors to consider when selecting a POS for a food truck:

- Connectivity and processes when offline
- Equipment or startup fees
- Ongoing monthly subscription or service fees
- Payment-processing fees
- Processing speed (how quickly does the money reach your bank account)
- Customer service and how quickly their tickets are resolved
- Ease of use, by both sales associate and customer
- Anticipated regulation changes

Further integrations and systems are available through some POS providers. Loyalty programs, payroll, and tax reporting are now available through some programs. Keep in mind that some of those added features may come with additional fees, so that should be considered before turning on the feature or deciding on a POS. At its core, the POS should allow payment processing and be able to produce revenue reports. Beyond that, additional services can be considered if they provide value or reduce other waste or expenses.

Theft/Security

The concept of fraud or the fear of theft could be alarming to a business owner, but there are steps that can be taken to prevent both. Common categories of fraud are: asset misappropriation, financial-statement fraud, and corruption. Asset misappropriation is the most common, making up 90 percent of all fraud cases.[17] This is when an employee steals or exploits company resources such as money, time, or product. Corruption or financial-statement fraud are much less common but should be prevented when possible, by creating an environment that is transparent and armed with checks and balances. There should always be a second person to double-check the activity and reports. For a solo entrepreneur, that person may be a bookkeeper, accountant, or auditor. The act of having published processes for checks and balances may also protect the person who most often manages resources.

Before getting any further on this topic, it is important to note two things. One is that (almost) every retail

---

17 "Six Strategies for Fraud Prevention in Your Business." Cg Tax, Audit & Advisory. February 11, 2019. Accessed April 12, 2019. https://www. cgteam.com/six-strategies-for-fraud-prevention-in-your-business/.

and restaurant business, that has employees, expects some theft or loss. It may be best to plan for a small percent of products that grow feet each month and chalk it up to the cost of doing business. Right or wrong, minor theft of products is prevalent and often happens without any ill-intention meant to the owner or business. Many people simply forgot to pick up milk that morning, so they bring home a nearly-empty gallon as they leave the kitchen. Or they are self-compensating for being expected to cover the extra hours since someone screwed up and the job must be done, so they take home a few orders of dinner for their waiting family. The point is, theft does not always appear under the mask of a disgruntled employee that is out for leveling a playing field or causing duress. And so the second note to mention is that many owners prefer to prevent theft or suspicion of theft rather than having to live through the process of managing the later fallout. It is zero fun for either party to navigate the proper steps when theft is suspected.

Steps for preventing theft by employees:

1. Know Your Employees

Changes in attitude or in the financial status of employees are reasons to be cautious. Even if the employees are well liked and trusted, or especially because they are, the owner or manager should be more aware during such times. Theft is often motivated by desperation or spite. If employees suddenly feel unappreciated or undervalued, they will be more likely to close that gap by cushioning their hours or taking cash and supplies. Similarly, if employees are making the tough decisions related to the basic needs of their family, they may misappropriate resources simply to ease the pain at home.

2. Make Employees Aware

Rather than dealing with a situation after it occurs, make it difficult to steal and easy to fear the likelihood of being caught. Everyone should be encouraged to report suspicion of theft. Employees are not the only people that can cause theft and security issues for a business. It could be a neighboring business, vendor, customer, or passerby that recognizes an opportunity. Rewarding employees for reporting suspicious activity can be more advantageous than rewarding them for periods without discovered loss or theft.

3. Implement Internal Controls

Documentation and tracking resources can prevent internal theft. Be clear on what should happen if there is inventory left over after a service shift. Food-service businesses should have processes defined for how food is safely stored, when products are donated to other organizations, or when employees can assume possession of it. Every retail business should have processes in place for handling money. Consider who will deposit cash and how the drawer is handled when that person is not present. Someone should be responsible for comparing deposits and drawer reports to the POS reports.

Anticipating the Losses and Planning for Wins

There is no better way to cause frustration and experience feelings of inadequacies as a business owner than to put the business in a precarious financial position. A long, hard day becomes almost unbearable when a food truck owner is faced with financial hardships and is struggling with how to keep the business moving forward. Creativity falls to side, and accidents become a common way of life when financial burdens steal the focus of a small-business owner. To avoid such a position, it is important to plan for financial upsets. Consider what would happen if the truck were out of service for a week, a series of weather storms were to roll through, a key employee was to fall ill, or a publicity nightmare were to occur. Are the business's financials strong enough to sustain such a downturn in revenue? Or what can be done to prepare for such a time, since downturns are inevitable? There should be plans in place that can be enacted when triggered. Trying to find the solutions when experiencing the downturn can be challenging because the manager is also dealing with whatever caused the resulting financial pain.

On the other hand, what should be done with the cash realized by a big financial win? Some businesses that do not have a plan in place will burn through the additional revenue without much thought or effort. Starting reserve accounts for future maintenance, pursuit of opportunities, or operational needs is a natural place to move unexpected revenue surpluses. Some businesses may also have a plan to reward employees or stakeholders when such a win happens. By making employees aware of that plan, a business owner may incentivize them with performance bonuses to put in the extra effort to create the winning formula. Perhaps most important during an uptick of revenue is to recognize what caused it and create a plan for replicating that environment.

Chapter Eight

Creating the Framework

Whether a business is self-funded or funded by other means, a business plan is a powerful tool for keeping everyone involved on the same page and focused on a realistic road map. Many business owners may continue to update the original business plan, which evolves into a growth plan as time continues after startup. The creation of a business plan can also help entrepreneurs evaluate objectively if they should move forward with opening the business as planned, modify the plan to be more profitable or sustainable, or simply walk away from it and chalk it up to a learning experience. Not every business idea is meant to become a business. Keeping that in mind may help entrepreneurs to evaluate the findings of research and financial projections objectively.

Business plans can vary drastically from one to the next. They do not need to be long but do need to include the pertinent information to act as a framework for the startup and early business stages. Ultimately, the plan should identify the customer need that is being met by the business, outline how the business would be structured and operated, and set expectations of and for its stakeholders. Common sections of a business plan include an executive brief, biographies of the owners and key personnel, operation plan, marketing plan, financial plan, market research, and a detailed description of key products or services along with their specifications and pricing. When producing a business plan, an entrepreneur may find value in meeting with subject-matter experts such as an attorney, finance professional, marketer, real-estate or equipment professional, and insurance broker. It is also common to have candid conversations with other people who already work or own businesses in the same space as the business that is being planned. The author of a business plan quickly becomes a sponge for information and then is challenged to decipher which data is relevant and may directly apply to the planning of such business.

When you sit down to write a business plan, it may help to first identify what is driving the interest in starting the business and then make a list of dreams or goals and a list of deal-breakers. Consider what you want to achieve with the business and what you are willing pay or sacrifice to reach those goals. The motivations and limitations are crucial to identify and will vary for each business, since personal values must be accounted for. The executive summary will be the last part of the business plan written, though it is usually presented at the start of the plan. That is because it will be a summary of all the findings and the shape of the business may change as the planning process happens. Tim Berry, a contributor here at Small Business Trends, is the founder of Palo Alto Software. He asked thousands of their business planning software users, to complete a survey about their businesses. The results led to a conclusion that people with a business plan where twice as likely to obtain capital or grow their businesses, than their counterparts who did not have a formal business plan.[18] The following sections describe the common categories of a business plan. However, the format of each business plan can be customized to fit the business.

18 Lesonsky, Rieva. "A Business Plan Doubles Your Chances for Success, Says a New Survey." Small Business Trends. January 20, 2016. Accessed March 21, 2019. https://smallbiztrends.com/2010/06/business-plan-success-twice-as-likely.html.

Biographies

Biographies of the owners and key personnel can add value to the business plan if it will be presented to a lender. Writing them may also identify specific weaknesses or strengths of the management team. For instance, if nobody's biography includes areas of culinary skill, financial management, legal expertise, HR management, or technical maintenance, then those gaps may need to be filled by third parties or employees. This is a prime time to evaluate the strength of the leadership team. Many business leaders consider people more important than any commodity of the business. That can be stressed even further for a food truck, which often relies on a lean team of people without much depth to cover when someone is absent.

Operations

The operational plan should clearly define how the business functions daily. Consider how resources will be sourced, produced, and distributed. For a food truck, this section should describe how food supplies will be ordered and where they will be stored. It will also define the process for preparing food products for distribution and where they will be sold. Locations could include regular service locations, such as food deserts or areas that have high foot traffic during meal times. It will be important to identify processes for quality control, performance evaluations, and basic function fulfillment. This section should also define who is working on the business, performing such roles as accounting, bookkeeping, human-resource management, marketing, and general business management. What and who does the business need to meet its goals? It would be advantageous to identify a timeline for startup and for milestones throughout the first one to two years. After reading this section, someone should be able to understand the premise of the business and its goals, how business owners are going to achieve those goals, and how the progress will be evaluated.

Research

Market research was conducted to understand the environment the business will be in, and that should be explained in depth. The research should combat common misperceptions and should lend to the goals set forth. It is likely that significant discoveries will be uncovered during the research process, and those should be brought to light in the business plan. Research can be conducted inexpensively through interviewing people in the industry, reading scholarly or popular material, or holding focus groups. To keep the business plan digestible, it may be appropriate to summarize findings and then include addendums or references as necessary.

Product

Products and services that will generate revenue for the business should be described in detail. That may include the menu(s) and products that create additional revenue lines, such as sauces, valued-added product, or hosted-catering services. Explain what the product is and why it fits the market it will be distributed to. Even though special menu items may be introduced periodically, the core menu of products should be identified and justified in this section. Some people may find it helpful to refine this section after testing a menu with a focus group or other audience. Presentation matters in this type of business, so be sure to address how menu items will be packaged or presented to the customer.

Marketing

The marketing plan should include a SWOT analysis, the marketing cycle, and specific plans for advertising and promotion. Remember the Four P's: product, place, price, and promotion. Within the SWOT, strengths and weaknesses will be unique to the business, while opportunities and threats could apply to similar businesses. Target markets should be described. Consider how people will learn about the business and its products, what the purchasing process looks like, and what value will be perceived. This is also an opportunity to set goals for how many people will be reached by your marketing communications—and how frequently. Refer to Chapter Six for an in-depth explanation of creating the marketing plan and how to execute it for a food truck.

Financials

Financial documents are the backbone of a business. While some entrepreneurs will enjoy the process of creating and analyzing financial projections, others may fear this process, either due to lack of experience or simply due to their personal interests. Templates are available online or through business-development organizations, and they can help an entrepreneur to skip the process of creating such forms from scratch. Some may prefer to work with accounting software such as QuickBooks to produce such projections and even run a mock year of accounting to get their arms around the numbers. In addition to a cash-flow pro forma, the entrepreneur should account for where the money is coming from to fund the startup and future cash needs. Lenders will appreciate seeing repayments of any loans on the cash-flow projection. Identify the break-even point, financial goals, and backup plans. Banks used to ask for three to five years of financial projections during the underwriting process of a loan, but most lenders now focus on the first one to three years. The heightened focus on earlier years may be because most businesses will pivot dramatically during the early years as opportunities are realized. It could also be because many businesses will not make it past three years, so there is more focus on if the business will be likely to survive and thrive during its very early years. Does the business have enough capital to support its plan and the probable deviations? And are business owners prepared to manage the finances appropriately, including cash flow? Refer to Chapter Seven for detailed descriptions of financial-planning processes and documents. Financial-projection templates are available as addendums.

Human-Resources Management

HR is a section that should be addressed even if the startup does not plan to immediately hire regular employees. If there will be services performed by the owners or their families, they will be addressed in this section. For companies planning to hire employees, it will be important to create a plan for hiring, training, retaining, and evaluating performance of employees. Throughout many communities, there is a war for hourly workers, and that is creating great frustration and cost for small businesses.

Regulations mandate the basic requirements of an employer. Some communities require health forms to be completed by everyone working in a food business. All businesses must comply with labor regulations including but not limited to wages, safe environments, and equal opportunity. Every employer will need to report wages and provide required insurances such as workers' compensation and unemployment. The direct costs of employees' wages are approximately 150 percent of their gross wages, because of the additional tax and insurance fees. Businesses should also budget for bookkeeping costs for processing payroll and reports.

Setting clear expectations of the employer and the employee will help eliminate some of the common frustrations while increasing retention and production. Providing employees with a manual and code of conduct can help everyone stay on the same page. Two of the most common complaints and reasons for leaving a company are lack of communication from management and lack of opportunities for growth. Managers can create a plan to combat both of those complaints before they become present in their company. Regular feedback can be more helpful to an employee than annual reviews, though it is important to have time designated to exchange performance reviews and evaluate compensation. The hourly wage may vary from one market to another, but the competitive wage for hourly wage workers is climbing, according to Donna Hood Crecca, a Principal of the research company, Technomic.[19] Expect wages to continue to increase if the demand for employees continues its recent trends. Some companies simply do not have enough employees and struggle to get enough employees to conduct their business. That also means that while some food-truck owners would like to be open for more shifts during a week, they may not be able to until they have excelled at recruiting, training, and retaining employees.

Insight: Principal at Technomic

Donna Hood Crecca is a principal at Technomic, the well-known and respected research company under the Winsight Media umbrella. Donna and I met while we were speakers at a national conference for convenience retailers. A few things she said stuck with me and now seem essential to share with food truck owners, so I asked for her input when writing this book.

There is a war for talent happening now as

---

19 Donna M Crecca, interview by Kay-Tee Olds, Phoenix, AZ, February 23, 2018.

employers try to attract and retain hourly workers. Supermarkets, quick-service restaurants, convenience stores, food trucks, and discount stores are all vying for a similar customer at times and almost always battling for the same employee. Those same employees could be the best arsenal for waging a continued battle, since 74 percent of c-store employees would be willing to recommend their employer to a friend.[20] For food-truck owners struggling to find more employees, a dollar spent on advertising through current employees may be a well-spent dollar.

Once an employee is hired, the work does not stop. Without offering perks and purpose beyond the competitive (and rising) salary, hourly employers will struggle to stay staffed. Employees are looking for work-life balance, training and advancement programs, flexible hours, bonus incentives, and a company that shares their personal values. The key reasons Donna shared that employees leave their jobs at C-stores could be like why employees leave food trucks. They find more appealing opportunities that address the issues that bother them: lack of predictability, not enough hours, and not enough benefits.

Low unemployment, a shrinking labor pool, and increased wages are making it more challenging for employers to find and keep good employees. Strategies should be created to increase retention. The cost to attract and retain employees can be costly

---

20 Crecca, Donna M. "Win the War for Talent." Convenience Retail University, Phoenix, AZ, February 21, 2018. Presented. Lecture.

for businesses that employ hourly workers, and that cost increases when high turnover is present.

Since recruitment and retention of employees is a significant challenge for many food-service businesses, employers are getting creative with their tactics. They may offer staying bonuses during their peak season or similar bonuses related to punctuality. Others are offering incentives related to continuing education and advancement opportunities. And some are providing performance bonuses based on the success of the overall business season, since front-line employees can greatly affect the results of a day or event. Still, employees cannot be forced to stay with an employer, so it is important to keep a close eye on changes in their performance and their attitude toward performing their tasks.

Other Considerations

After creating most of the business plan, it is time to step back, review it, and consider if it is enough. Chances are, the research or financial projections may have uncovered a need for expanding on additional opportunities or a need to address some of the threats or weaknesses before deciding to start the business. After taking those questions into consideration, an additional section can be added to the business plan, or the author can go back and update the related sections. A business plan is often a liquid document that will continue to experience changes as time continues, and the plan can be refined.

Some areas for expanding on opportunities could be

related to generating additional streams of revenue. Most food-truck owners realize at some point that their overhead costs do not change, or not by much, when they increase the volume of service shifts or customers that a truck serves. Increasing the use of such capital equipment, marketing efforts, and licenses could diminish the pressure on a unit of product to realize a state of break-even or profit. Other purveyors may realize that they can greatly increase their total revenue and bottom-line profit by upselling customers with products that complement their core offering, such as sauces, beverages, or seasoning packets. Other considerations for pursuing revenue could come in the off season and not be connected to the operation of a food truck. For solo entrepreneurs who are self-employers and do not employee other people, they may find that the numbers start to make a lot more sense when they only rely on food-truck profit for a portion of their annual income. Rather than trying to live off six months of owners' draws for an entire year, especially in regions where food trucks do not commonly operate during winter months, some business owners will account for a shutdown period and work another job during that time.

The entrepreneur may have discovered methods to save cost or minimize risk. For instance, there may have been new realizations that uncovered lending opportunities that come with better repayment terms, or perhaps there is a grant that the business could apply for. Otherwise, the owners may have produced the business plan and then started considering how they could take such a plan to other like-minded people to find partners or even businesses to team with; both options could reduce their personal financial risk and investment.

Each section of the business plan is intermingled with another. Think of a business like a Rubik's cube; as one section connects, another may fall out of alignment. The startup process is a puzzle that requires much strategy and continuous twists and turns, until the right combination of moves leads to that aha moment and the business can be started sustainably.

Exit Plan

Surprisingly to some, many people do not consider their exit plan before starting a business. Lenders and business consultants may look for this in a business plan because it helps to identify what sort of value the entrepreneur expects to pull from the business, what their end goals are, and where their limits are. "A typical business owner misjudges the value of a company by 59 percent."[21]. Some people are better at starting businesses, while others are best at managing or growing them. Consider which person you are before starting a business. The exit strategy of the owner will have a direct correlation to the type of startup funding that would be appropriate. For instance, an entrepreneur who wants to start a business and not experience the cash-flow burden of repayment during its first year may be the ideal candidate for a deferred or

---

21 "MassMutual Business Owner Perspectives Study." MassMutual. 2012. Accessed March 21, 2019. https://www.massmutual.com/mmfg/pdf/small_business_factsheet_women.pdf.

graduated loan that is secured by business-owned collateral. In that case, the business would either need to be sold as a value-added package, for a higher amount than the money invested, or it would need to scale enough to cover the larger repayments down the road. Shockingly, 88 percent of business owners do not have an exit plan.[22]

Exiting the business may be triggered by a predetermined factor, or it may happen when either the business or person does not want to continue the current path. A predetermined factor may still happen at unexpected times, as it could be an offer from someone to purchase the business or it could be triggered by a significant swing of a market. In that case, food truck owners may commit to exiting the business if their expenses ever doubled their revenue for two consecutive quarters. Or they may set the limit at two consecutive years of loss. Or the plan could be to sell as soon as the startup costs are repaid and the business shows enough profit to match the average salary of two people in the business. Whatever the trigger is, it should be identified, and part of that means being honest with yourself about how much you are willing to risk or how much you are willing to bail out a company during a downtown or slow start. It could be helpful for entrepreneurs to set a list of triggers so they can objectively evaluate each situation as it occurs, and they can evaluate whether the business should be winded down or they should exit the business because it will be led or owned by someone else.

---

22 Rogerson, Andrew. "Selling a Business in 2018 is Still Bullish." Rogerson Business Services. June 28, 2018. Accessed April 15, 2019. https://www.rogersonbusinessservices.com/selling-a-business-in-2018-is-still-bullish/.

Exiting a business can be a glorious, triumphant moment when the mission set forth at startup is realized. Or it can be a process that involves moments of sorrow, regret, and self-doubt, if the business is being closed because it is not sustainable to continue operating. And sometimes there is simply a status-quo middle ground that is experienced when the business did what it was intended to, ran its course, and will cease to exist rather than pivoting into a new business cycle, which would involve reinventing, growing, and maturing all over again.

Close It

Shutting down a business is the last strategy a lender will want to hear, but that is sometimes the best route for exiting a business. This strategy is basically the non-strategy, except in the case of a business that was planned to operate during a short-term need in the market. It is usually what happens when a business gets to a point that it realizes its brand and inventory have little or no value to anyone else, or the continuation of the business is being disrupted by an external force that would require significant investment to overcome. This exit process is often coupled with a sense of defeat experienced by the owner or leadership team, who likely tried to build or grow a business but could not generate the momentum needed to do so. When shutting down a business, the owners should notify all vendors, suppliers, and government entities they work with or report to. It is also best practice to notify employees directly, as well as key customers. Some businesses will keep the closing of a business a secret in hopes their employees do not leave before the final day of business. Others may provide incentives to keep them working until the business wraps up its final dealings and can be closed without lingering liabilities.

Drain It

Often easier than selling a business in its entirety is the method of draining the business. This is ideal for an owner who wants to capture profits while exiting, without the planning and work that may be required of selling it. Basically, the owner continues to pull profit or excess revenue from the business while liquidating equipment, real estate, and inventory with the plan of depleting the business. Sometimes an owner will realize during this process that they are still left with brand value, digital assets, or intellectual property that can be monetized as they complete the exiting process. A disadvantage of this strategy can be taxation, if too much of the business is drained during the same fiscal or calendar year.

Sell It

The process of selling is common for a successful business that generates regular profit or holds a strong balance sheet. This may present the greatest return on investment, often in the form of capital gains for food trucks. The owner may sell all or part of the business when exiting. The sale could include any or all assets and goodwill or reputation. Valuating a small business can be tricky since the business can sometimes command a price different than what a traditional valuation method would dictate. It will sometimes depend on what a buyer is willing to pay. Finding the right buyer can be like dating in the sense that each party is trying to figure out if the other is the right person to be working with, when they previously knew nothing or little about each other. Owners who plan to sell the business as their exit strategy should start compiling appropriate documents and recording everything three to five years before the exit is to occur. Financial documents, liens or loans, warranties and receipts for equipment, employment records, and proof of licenses or permits are important to have available. Many licenses or permits for a food truck operation will not be transferrable, and that would be important to disclose. Rather than selling an entire business, a food truck owner may decide to sell parts of the business, such as the equipment or contracts. In other cases, not common to food trucks, owners may decide to create an IPO and take the company public, which removes their ownership stake but may have other financial advantages. It is recommended that a buyer and seller both consult their own legal advisors during the sale of a business. Seventy-five percent of business owners who sold reported having post-exit remorse.[23] Planning for such an exit strategy can help the seller remain objective during the process.

---

23 "State of Owner Readiness." Exit Planning Institute. 2013. Accessed March 21, 2019. http://www.exit-planning-institute.org/wp-content/uploads/2015/05/State-of-Owner-Readiness-Survey-2013-Presentation.pdf.

Friendly Sale

Different than a traditional sale of a business is a friendly buyout, because it often means that a person(s) will buy a business without the full song and dance of selling to an investor or otherwise unknown buyer. Family members or friends may want to buy a food truck business because they know enough about the owner or the business to feel comfortable taking it over, sometimes even when the business does not show the records or documents that it otherwise would need to for a traditional investment buyer. Sometimes a friendly buyer comes in the form of an employee or partner. If a partner is buying out the other partner(s), ideally those terms and processes were identified in the partnership operating agreement. When employees buy the business through a friendly buying process, it may be because they want to continue the business when the owner wants to be finished with it or because they are able to when the owner is no longer able to operate the business. Many creative payoff solutions can be created during a friendly buyout, and it is important to identify what exactly is to happen for the transfer of liability and equity and at what point ownership transfers. It also saves much headache or court time to predetermine what happens if payment, transfer, or operation is not executed as agreed upon. Everything should be in writing, to protect all parties and the business.

Merge It

A CMI Research study found that out of the business owners surveyed, 87 percent did not have a documented exist or transition plan despite that 96 percent expressed it is important to have one. [24] That is unfortunate because doing so is a valid exit plan when opportunities arise. A business may be interested in acquiring another business to increase the value of their current operation. Mergers and acquisitions are commonly inspired by a desire to dramatically increase market share, either by acquiring another brand's customers or eliminating a strong competitor. Another reason for a merger or acquisition may be that the two businesses' products or services are stronger together than apart. For instance, restaurant owners may want to merge with a food-truck business rather than starting their own truck operation. Instead of the restaurant owners starting the food truck from scratch, they may merge with the truck, and sometimes that means that the owner of the food truck would still be present in operating it but not working on the business financials or management any longer. Other times, one of the businesses will simply consume the other and remove key leaders.

Executive Summary

Writing an effective executive summary often requires that it be written last, after the business plan is constructed.

---

24 "Planning for Business Transition." Baker Tilly. 2014. Access on April 12, 2019. https://www.bakertilly.com/uploads/planning-for-business-transition.pdf.

This section should be placed at the beginning of the business plan to summarize key findings from research and highlight significant elements of the business. It should help the reader understand why the business should succeed, at a glance. If there are common concerns about the business leader, the type of business, or the industry it will reside in, the executive summary should address them, so the reader can see beyond them before diving into the meat of the plan.

Think of the executive summary as a shortened version of the business plan. In case some are not willing or able to read through the entire plan, be sure the summary has enough depth to help them follow the thought process of the plan and realize the value of the business that is to be started. If you want anyone to read through the rest of the plan, the executive summary must draw them in.

Mission, Vision, Values

Like the executive summary, it may be easiest to refine the mission, vision, and value statements after writing the business plan. The general concept of such statements may have been considered before constructing the plan, but the vision of what the business would look like and what it would mean to its stakeholders was vague until it was further formed by decisions made after research and during the compilation of a business plan. The mission statement clearly defines why the business exists and what it does. The vision statement is what will be realized if the mission is achieved. The value statement is written either as a sentence or a list that recognizes which core values cannot be comprised, even at an opportunity to advance the mission. Some entrepreneurs will list their mission, vision, and values within the executive summary, while others will create a separate section for this information. In the future, such key information can be shared with customers and employees.

Chapter Nine

Fund the Vision

Common misperceptions may lead someone to fear that half of all startups will not make it past their first birthday. However, it is 30 percent of small businesses that fail in their first year, according to Investopedia. The other 20 percent get to that 50 percent failure rate between years two and five.[25] Either way, the odds are not pretty, and that is exactly why it is so important for a business owner to continuously learn how to become a stronger business owner and leader. One of the primary reasons that businesses fail in their first year, or even initial five years, is poor management of capital. Properly funding your startup business will allow you to focus on other key performance indicators that could make or break it, such as filling a need in the market, building the right team, and focusing on the customer.

Think of funding a business like feeding a child. Without access to the right foods, a child will struggle to learn, adapt, and grow to be a contributing member

---

25 "Top 6 Reasons New Businesses Fail." Investopedia. Accessed April 12, 2019. https://www.investopedia.com/slide-show/top-6-reasons-new-businesses-fail/.

of society. All the same applies to funding a business. An organization with limited or inadequate funding may still achieve great things, but it is less likely to do so without encountering unnecessary obstacles.

Types of Capital

There are four basic types of funding that a food truck should consider: *seed*, *startup*, *mezzanine*, and *bridge*. Perhaps the most difficult to secure will be the seed and startup capital, since the business does not have a financial history, and many food truck owners lack some of the other preferred credentials of a borrower. Rather than going through the process of finding, applying, and securing funding, some entrepreneurs will decide to simply use personal funds to finance a startup. However, there are numerous reasons that a business may be better served by securing outside funding for at least some of its cash needs.

Seed: This money may be needed for research and planning phases before the business moves into startup mode.

Startup: This money is used for purchasing initial needs for opening day and funding the cash-flow gaps during the first year.

Mezzanine: This money is used during growth phases. It could be used to buy additional food trucks, updated equipment, or anything else needed to grow to a larger scale.

Bridge: This money is used for short-term needs, usually between startup and mezzanine funds. This could be credit lines, credit cards, short-term loans, or similar short-term solutions that would be repaid when the longer-term loan is funded, usually with more favorable repayment terms than bridge capital.

Funding Sources

Money may not grow on trees, but it can be found in so many places. Some entrepreneurs will only consider traditional loans through their bank, which are secured by collateral and repaid in regular monthly payments. That is a common route for many small loans, but there are so many sources to consider when deciding what funding source is best for a startup business.

Business Loan: Banks and credit unions can be skeptical of startup businesses, especially those led by inexperienced business owners or those that reside in a risky industry, which often defines the food truck startup. Personal financial statements will be required and usually collateral as well. This would be a traditional funding method for a small-business startup.

Guaranteed Loan: The Small Business Administration (SBA) has several programs to guarantee loans for small businesses, making it easier and less risky for a lender to fund a startup. Microloans require that the lender provide business training and support to the borrower in exchange for the SBA backing the loan, which can be up to $35,000 with up to six-year repayment terms. SBA Express loans can be much faster than microloans, with approval in 36 hours, and can be for amounts up to $150,000; but SBA only guarantees 50 percent of it, so the lender would be responsible for the rest. Some cities have business centers that specialize in connecting people, especially women and minorities, to training and guaranteed loans.

Home-Equity Loan: This is a relatively easy and quick way to fund a business. The responsibility falls on the shoulders of the business owner, whose house is collateral for the loan. There are usually fees to process such a loan, and it would be considered a personal debt. This is only an option if the entrepreneur, or someone investing in the business, has adequate equity in a home.

Credit Cards: It is common for small businesses to use credit cards as a regular funding source because they are such a quick and easy solution to access. Such funding could be appropriate when short-term credit is needed to buy products this week for sales that happen next week. However, some businesses try to fund their startup process on a credit card or look to such sources for covering cash-flow problems. This form of funding can compound the issues, though.

Personal Funds: Consider that some of the startup cost of a business is usually derived from personal funds. However, it would not be wise for business owners to deplete their cash reserves during the initial startup process to fund the entire business this way because it would weaken their personal financial statement and remove a potential source of future cash injections. Remember that it takes a while to turn a regular profit from a food truck, so personal funds may be needed to sustain personal expenses during that time leading toward realizing a profit.

Private Investor: Some aspiring business owners are fortunate to know a private investor or know someone who knows someone who knows a private investor. Others rely on third-party brokers to connect them with a direct investor. An advantage to this route is that it could reduce the initial personal investment of the entrepreneur. However, that usually comes at the cost of either part of the business ownership or a larger interest rate. When working with a private investor, it is important to evaluate how much comfort exists between the parties.

Partnership: When two or more people want to join forces collectively, sharing the responsibilities and rewards of owning a business, the company is often setup as a partnership. The cash needs during startup are spread among the partners as well as the work, unless an operating agreement calls for other arrangements. Creating a partnership is a valid route for entrepreneurs looking to overcome a shortcoming. For instance, a natural partnership for a food truck could be in one person with a strong culinary background and the other with experience managing a small business. Sometimes an entrepreneur who is light on cash, or access to it, will seek an operating or silent partner.

Friends and Family: This route may seem easy to some people but remember that conversation at the Thanksgiving table will change dramatically. Aunt Sue will want to know how her investment is performing. All is well when it works out as planned but borrowing from friends and family can go awry quickly, especially when it is managed too loosely, without written terms and payback options. A written agreement can be prepared by a lawyer. Answer the question, "What happens if it does not go as planned?"

Crowdfunding: Growing in popularity, this source of funding is gaining attention and becoming more regulated. There are sites such as Kickstarter, Indiegogo, Kiva, and GoFundMe that facilitate the ask for money and the exchange of money between the dreamer and supporters. Some crowdfunding options—like Kiva—act as loans, with various lenders, while others—like Kickstarter—act more as a presale platform. When setting up a public crowdfunding campaign, it is important to use emotional tools such as video and to present the product's benefits clearly. The process of crowdfunding $5,000 may take 30 days to 120 days, to create the campaign, prepare communication, and then let it run its course.

Grants: Some entrepreneurs qualify for grants because of their socio-economic status, where they are located, or other factors determined by grant committees. Grants are funds that are given to an organization or person to move a project forward, without the expectation of payback. There usually needs to be a common interest being served. Common places to seek grants are local economic-development programs, federal grant programs, trade associations, and corporations whose interests you may be serving. The process can be lengthy, with the application and approval process often taking up to twelve months and then an additional couple of months for disbursement of funds.

Getting the Money

Plan for delays and start early to access seed or startup funds before they are needed. In some cases, entrepreneurs may need to take out short-term personal loans to access the funds sooner than they will arrive from a business loan, and then repay them once the business funds are received. Just about every source of funding will take surprisingly longer than anticipated. It can take up to six months from application to funding when using an SBA-guaranteed loan. Even unsecured business loans for food-truck startups can take up to three months after applying, meeting with loan officers, giving your entire life's history to underwriters, closing on the loan, and waiting for disbursement. Grants can take up to a year to be disbursed. Crowdfunding and personal gifts from friends or family may be a little faster but remember it will take some time and skill to prepare the materials needed for such a process to run smoothly and not become a full-time distraction from starting the business.

Tips for Pitching

People buy from people, so expect that a lender or grantor will want to meet with you in person when you are asking for funds to start a business. It can be intimidating for someone who is not versed in asking for money or someone who fears rejection. What is the worst that can happen, though? Someone says no? Then refine the pitch and go ask someone else. Whether pitching a bank, economic-development team, or an investor, here are some tips for making the pitch:

1. Make the appointment with a decision maker.
2. Dress business formal; do not go straight from a morning of prep at the kitchen.
3. Bring the business plan and all financial documents.
4. Remember to address what they will get out of being your funding source.
5. Be confident and own it! Do not waver.
6. State how much you are personally investing. That shows skin in the game.

7. Above all else, be honest. The goal is to find the right fit, not take the first offer.
8. Be prepared to answer questions about the business plan and your personal financial status.
9. Plan your pitch and include a story that answers the *why* question.
10. Be cognizant of time. If you are unsure, ask how much time someone has.

Before making the pitch, consider practicing with someone. If you have built an advisory team, this could be a good opportunity to lean on them for experience and advice. Pitching is an art form, and someone who has little or no experience will benefit from practicing and receiving feedback. The pitch can matter just as much as what is on paper. Investors and lenders commonly report that they are judging the person as much as the content. They may be looking to answer the simple question of whether they think that person has what it takes to make this work.

Why Banks Say No

Startups are risky businesses for a bank to support. Consider the failure rates, lack of operating history, and lack of income that business represents. However, it can be done. Obtaining a substantial business loan from a bank or credit union usually requires that the owner support it with a strong personal financial statement or collateral, that the person applying for the loan have history with the bank or paying back startup loans, or that there is another party guaranteeing part of the loan. It may become easier to obtain lines of credit or traditional loans once the business has been operating and showing steady income, but the funding process of a startup is another whole story. Even though traditional loans may be difficult to secure at reasonable terms for a food truck, obtaining one may create opportunities for future lines of funding.

When approaching a bank, credit union, or other lender, consider ways to reduce their risk. What is it about you or your business that is less risky than the next business or the last food truck that applied for funding? Be prepared to justify why an investment in the food truck is safer or better for the lender than saying no.

Tips for Crowdfunding

Crowdfunding is a new method for funding a small-business startup, at least in comparison with the history of standard business loans. There can be advantages to this method, since anyone can be eligible regardless of credit history or personal assets. Another advantage is that some crowdfunding solutions are set up so there is an exchange of value immediately, rather than repayment in cash. For instance, a food truck entrepreneur may ask for $25 contributions in exchange for a $25 gift card or branded T-shirt. But some platforms act more as a loan with several lenders, so the business would need to repay the loaned amount in addition to fees associated. Most public asks for money involve the use of emotional triggers, often driven by sharing a story with an audience who cares about it. The following five tips may clarify lingering questions.

1. **Select a platform:** Kickstarter, Indiegogo, and GoFundMe are examples of sites that manage crowdfunding campaigns. Each has its own rules and fees, so pick the solution that fits your needs.
2. **Watch other campaigns** and participate in some: Learn from others to apply techniques that you liked and avoid mistakes that you noticed.
3. **Create video:** An emotional appeal can be best conveyed to strangers via video. Videos are common elements of successful campaigns.
4. **Sell. Sell. Sell.** This is not a "if you build it, they will come" form of raising funds. Self-promotion will be crucial, and it helps to have an army of friends and family that promote it as well.
5. **Pre-book dollars:** Just like nonprofits do when they host a gala and use peer pressure to drive donations, entrepreneurs can ask investors to lead the crowdfunding efforts by either matching contributions or simply setting a public example.

If the process of procuring funds is overwhelming and seems to be stunting the progress of moving toward opening day, it may be worth hiring someone to provide the service of acting on behalf of your business to secure funds. Or it may be time to consider bringing on a partner that balances your weaknesses with complementary strengths. Remember that the startup phase of a small business is not the time to focus on your personal growth. It may happen naturally, but an entrepreneur is often best served to focus on their strengths and hire their weaknesses.

Chapter Ten

Stop Before You Go

Think back to the moment when you found out your family was expanding, you started a new career, or you ventured out on your own for the first time. Did the journey unfold the way you envisioned? Did it turn out just like the role model's journey that you followed? Not likely. And that will hold true when starting a business. Think of the perfect business and someone you know who succeeded. You are not that person, and that is okay—in fact, it is perfect, since that person's story was already written. Starting a food truck from scratch means that you hold the brush and will soon procure the paints for an empty canvas. Many hands will touch it, and many eyes will judge it, but only you can decide when it is time to pivot and look at it from another angle.

Anyone can start a business, but not every business should be started. It is okay to back away from a business idea even after spending the time and energy to create the entire business plan. If it is not the right business or not the right time to start it, just tuck that plan away and chalk it up as a learning lesson. Often, a business idea that makes it through the startup process will look much different than how it was originally envisioned, and that is exactly why it is so important to conduct a thorough business-planning process.

Evaluate and Pivot

After creating a business plan, including its financial projections, ask yourself, "Does it make sense?" Even at a glance, something may jump off the pages as not being realistic or begging to be questioned. Imagine that you are reading the plan for the first time, or better yet, go share it with a stranger who will not care about protecting your feelings. Ask the questions an investor would.

1. Is there a likely return on investment?
2. When will I get paid from the business, and how much?
3. How much do I need to invest?
4. And how much more could be needed if that is not enough?
5. Who else is investing in the business?
6. What need does the product/service satisfy in the market?
7. Who is the direct competition, and how does this differ?
8. Who has already succeeded at this type of business, and how do we compare?
9. What is the exit strategy?
10. Why does this matter to me?

Photo Courtesy of: Eric Melton-White, "Vending is a family affair at Thai-Riffic Food Cart State St. Mall Madison, WI", May 2018.

For those who created a business plan while working through the previous chapters of this book, there were likely moments of revelation and pivots that happened throughout that work. Others may be looking at their financial projections and wondering how to decrease the risk or simply increase the revenue so they can realize a profit. If there was not a revelation or an obvious need to pivot during the planning process, it is time to seek help, because there are always ways that a business plan can be improved. Speaking with someone who was recruited to be a subject-matter expert to serve on your advisory board could shed a new light on the plan.

During the planning process, a timeline should have been defined. Does it still make sense? Some entrepreneurs can start such micro-businesses in less than two months, while it may take another person a year to have everything ready for launching a business. Either way, the timeline should keep the startup on track, as it is easy to get distracted by shiny objects or the excitement of a great win. Consider where the accountability comes from to get the business opened on a schedule and performing at its expected level. Solo entrepreneurs will sometimes create informal alliances with accountability buddies so that they can vocalize their plans and have someone who will expect progress reports. Others may hire a life or business coach to play that role.

Food trucks notoriously fall short on available cash during startup or the early years of operation, as evidenced by Chris Brockel, Operations Coordinator of FEED, a shared commercial kitchen that houses several food carts. He has observed food truck entrepreneurs making great sacrifices to then never see their business come to fruition. Given that information, examine the cash-flow budget with a fine-tooth comb and consider what is missing. Does it account for all those pesky details that are often overlooked when creating a budget? Properly funding a business will greatly determine whether it can sustain the hurdles it will inevitably face.

Keep the Bus Filled

The actions of other people may be the biggest gamble when starting a food truck. Think about how dependent the business is on the perception and action of other people, from the lender to the health inspector, to the customers who become critics, to the employees needed to scale the business. Bringing people along with you during startup can prove valuable for many reasons. An advisory board can be developed to keep the interest and gain the advice of subject-matter experts who have experience with insurance, legal, licensing, product development, human resources, or marketing. Customers can become brand ambassadors if provided the right tools and encouragement. And other businesses can become advocates and an extension of the sales efforts when cross-promotional partnerships are developed. The important thing to remember is that successful food trucks need a full bus. Even the food truck businesses that are operated solely by the entrepreneur need to find a way to expand their capacity and cover their weaknesses or discomforts.

Customer Experience

While it may seem obvious from a distance, it is sometimes too easy for a food truck operator to forget how important the customer experience is. Creating and driving the brand through all facets of the business should include the consideration of the full customer experience. The finer details can make all the difference. Knowing what you want the customer experience to be is important when designing the other components of the business, such as menu, staffing, location, and branding.

Benefits of providing a consistent customer experience can include increased loyalty, a higher average ticket, and a better likelihood of customers becoming ambassadors for the business. Treating customers with respect and reacting empathetically to their feedback can be important to remember during the rush of a lunch shift. As much as it is ego boosting and a pure joy to receive positive comments from customers, it is even more important to address the critiques provided by customers. Criticism can be productive if it is handled appropriately, since it allows the business an opportunity to turn that person into a customer for life and to improve employee training or processes.

Tips for developing good face-to-face customer relationships:

- Greet every customer in a timely and friendly manner, while acting within the brand.
- If there will be a longer-than-usual wait, convey that to the line of customers.
- Ask for feedback throughout the process. This could be as simple as asking customers how their experience is or asking if anything can be done to improve their visit.
- When customers share positive feedback, ask them to share that online as well. It not only spreads the word about the business but also leaves a stronger memory of the experience with that customer as they tell the story.
- Be sure all employees are trained to be front line. Even a back-of-house employee will interact verbally or through body language with the customer

at some point. Training can help ensure a positive interaction.

- Keep magic money around. I keep a $20 bill in key locations, and employees know that they have access to it at any time if they discover an opportunity to create a moment of magic for the customer. It could be hopping into a nearby shop to buy a birthday card or buying a supply off a nearby vendor if the customer requests a condiment or container that is not on board that day. It could mean feeding a parking meter nearby for a customer who is in line longer than planned. Opportunities to go that extra step often leave a lasting impression with a customer.

- Create a game out of finding new ways to provide stellar service. Employees can compete or work together to receive rewards for documenting new ways that they extended the brand and created a memorable customer experience.

Elevator Pitch

Procuring the needed resources to give the business a healthy start often involves pitching the idea to other people in a way that conveys the value without diluting the significant factors with irrelevant information. That could be a traditional lender, a spouse that is vicariously involved, a grant-awarding committee, a business partner, or a key supplier who may be providing payment terms that are key to keeping the cash flow trucking along. An elevator pitch often starts that process. Every entrepreneur should have an elevator pitch—or series of elevator pitches, since there may be categories of stakeholders with significantly different reasons for taking interest in the business. When creating an elevator pitch, think about what you could say to a person while traveling in an elevator with them for one minute. Leading with your *why* can help people connect with your vision on an emotional level. Rather than explaining the fine features of a product or how you are sourcing supplies, focus on the benefits. Who is going to benefit from this business starting up, and why it should matter to them or other people? Do not forget the ask. Consider asking everyone for something. It can be surprising when the last person you would expect to ask for something reveals the right connection or ability to help you with your largest roadblocks. People usually enjoy helping other people, especially if they feel connected to their story. It would not be uncommon for a stranger to be the missing link when looking for a solution to a challenge. Lastly, be memorable. Remember that people say yes to people, not companies. Consider what it is about you or the way you present your elevator pitch that will help someone think of you days or weeks later. Those who own top-of-mind awareness will receive more response to their requests.

Triple Bottom Line

Evaluating a business, especially a young or very small business, can be full of challenges when considering a triple bottom line, which is an accounting framework that measures the social, environmental, and financial results of an organization. Much of the difficulty is purely from a lack of data that is specific to a company, but triple bottom line can still be considered during decision-making processes. People, planet, and profit make up the triple bottom line. Larger businesses—those that can track specific economic impact or their pollution and environmental waste—may have an easier time evaluating and placing a report-card grade on their progress of creating a profitable bottom line for people and planet, but even small businesses can make decisions and create policies that move the needle in the right direction.

Consider what impact your company or its existence will have on other people. Will it create living-wage jobs, purpose, and a sense of satisfaction for its employees? Will customers find their lives or moments of their day improved because of your food truck? How about the community at large—what impact will your business have? A small business creating new jobs in a community is a big win for people if those employees are retained. In fact, according to the Small Business Administration (SBA), small businesses added 1.9 million net new jobs in 2018 and employs 47.5 percent of the country's private workforce.[26] Insert stat here about the economic impact of jobs created by small businesses. Businesses may also support social initiatives of employees or perform community service by donating products, dollars, or time to help other people.

Measuring a food truck's impact on the planet can

26 Theorux, Emily. "Small Business Drive Job Growth in the U.S." U.S. Small Business Administration. April 25, 2018. Accessed April 11, 2019. https://www.sba.gov/advocacy/small-businesses-drive-job-growth-us.

be very difficult, but there are some factors that could be measured easily and often with identified values that can be discovered through third-party research. Food trucks are mobile businesses that feed diners on the go, so they provide disposable containers and utensils to nearly every customer. They also consume energy to power their operation, move to various locations, and complete the food preparation and cleanup process. Additionally, food trucks that order supplies from a distance, often through a distributor, leave a larger carbon footprint than those who source locally when reasonably possible. Some managers are sourcing eco-friendly packaging to decrease their footprint. They may also be considering the impact of their power consumption when they design their apparatus and menu, adjusting the type of fuel to be appropriate for the level of consumption. Around every corner there are opportunities for food trucks to improve their report card for their impact on the planet, and many are embracing the chance to improve their triple bottom line.

Measuring the financial profit can be the most straightforward—and has long been the traditional—method to determine the health of an organization. Balance sheets and profit and loss statements are among the common tools used to measure the financial health of any business, including food trucks. Cash-flow projections can help a business to predict the future financial results, but financial accounting is most accurate when looking back to past results. A business may consider comparing quarter-to-quarter or year-to-year results to gauge whether their performance is improving. When reviewing such results, it can also be helpful to compare the results to industry norms, which can reveal a greater gap or achievement if the business is pacing with or against the industry trends.

The *four bottom lines* is another take on the triple bottom line that may help small business owners to get their arms around matters that seem more personal of relevant. This concept refers to evaluating the effect of the business on you, your family, your business, and your community. Like the triple bottom line, the four bottom lines can act as a conscious value-based framework for guiding decisions and evaluating performance.

Ready? Now Go.

If after conducting the research, creating the plan, speaking with advisors, and performing a smell test, the business presents as both feasible and likely profitable, then GO! It is time to run and start executing the plan. It can be easy and safe for an aspiring entrepreneur to get caught up in the planning process or distracted by the seemingly endless roadblocks that pop up along the way. The difference between a person with ideas and a person who takes control of their destiny by becoming an entrepreneur is the act of starting the business and becoming vulnerable to the shifting winds that will surround you.

No matter how much planning can be done prior to opening a food truck, the plan will continuously change, and it must adapt to new findings. This type of business is so small but so mighty if it stays nimble. The advantages of having a microbusiness, especially one that is owned by only one or two individuals, is that it can quickly pivot to cut losses when a product or location does not pan out, and partners can look to opportunities as they are discovered through a hands-on business-management approach. The disadvantages of such a small independently owned business are the same but with opposite results. It can be easy to forget about the plan entirely and get distracted by an opportunity of the day or to become so emotional about the personal attachment that it becomes impossible to remain objective or see the larger picture when reacting pragmatically to a challenge of daily operation.

The life cycle of a business is the same for food trucks as it is for any other retailer, manufacturer, or large or small business. It starts with the launch, which is often followed by the most rapid growth, sometimes for the first year or for several years. That rapid growth is often inspired by the ability of the organization to meet the need of its customers and to provide a new option to meet those needs. It is also fueled by the fact that previous performance indicators were absent or small due to the young nature of the business. Once the business stabilizes and discovers its point of least resistance in the scaling process, it enters a stage of maturity. Just like a teenager, an organization in that stage is still discovering new findings and adapting its appearance or reactions to better fit its values and society around it. Life is exciting as growth continues. At some point, the organization will plateau and then decline unless rebirth happens. During such a phase, a food truck business may seek to expand locations or products, grow into a brick-and-mortar, transition to a catering company, become a franchisor, or completely recreate its identity to better match the current trends and opportunities.

Entrepreneurs can spend more time with their business in its early days than they spend with any one person in their life. For that reason, if not for many other reasons, the process of starting and building a business, should be enjoyable. Finding ways to celebrate failures, and then celebrate the successes from the learning that occurred, can be lifesaving. Owning a food truck can be a wild ride that accelerates quickly, and that ride only starts once the truck is fueled.

Made in the USA
Columbia, SC
18 December 2020